List of Contents

Introduction: The Pathway to Long Lasting Wealth

In the realm of wealth and prosperity, where dreams and aspirations merge with numbers and strategies, we embark upon a journey that transcends the ordinary. Welcome to "The Art of Money: Strategies to Get, Maintain and Preserve the Wealth." I am both humbled and excited to be your guide through the labyrinth of fiscal intricacies, sharing insights forged from years of experience and an unwavering passion for the world of business and finance.

Imagine a canvas where every choice you make, every dollar you invest, and every decision you undertake paints a portrait of your financial destiny. This book is your palette, a symphony of wisdom and practicality, designed to empower you to sculpt a life that gleams with financial independence, purposeful investment, and enduring security.

Before we delve into the wealth of strategies that await within these pages, permit me to illuminate the purpose and promise of this odyssey.

A New Perspective on Wealth: Beyond Dollars and Cents
The pursuit of wealth often conjures images of opulence, luxury, and lavish indulgence. But beneath the surface glimmers a more profound truth. True financial mastery

extends beyond the accumulation of money; it resides in the art of creating value, of nurturing dreams, and of making a lasting impact on the lives of those around us.

Consider the tapestry of human existence, woven with threads of innovation, resilience, and aspiration. Each financial decision, whether grand or modest, contributes to the fabric of our collective prosperity. This prologue invites you to peer beyond the ordinary façade of wealth and embrace a perspective that illuminates the intricate interplay between personal success and the well-being of the global community.

The Essence of Financial Resilience
In a world fraught with uncertainties, financial resilience stands as an emblem of strength. The journey outlined in this book does not promise an absence of challenges; rather, it equips you with the tools to navigate them deftly. As we traverse the chapters ahead, we will delve into risk management, strategies for weathering economic storms, and methods of turning adversity into opportunity. After all, it is during the moments of greatest challenge that the seeds of lasting success are sown.

The Pathway Unveiled: Navigating the Book
Each chapter in this book is a gate to a realm of knowledge waiting to be explored. From the foundational principles that underpin wealth creation to the sophisticated strategies of investment, taxation, and legacy planning, we will

traverse the gamut of financial mastery. Each sub-chapter offers an intricate mosaic of key points, meticulously designed to be both informative and actionable.

Your Role in the Tapestry

As the reader, you are not merely an observer; you are an active participant in this journey. The insights you glean from these pages are seeds that, when nurtured with intention and action, can flourish into magnificent trees of financial achievement. The path to mastery requires dedication, adaptability, and the willingness to continually expand your horizons.

Now, with the foundation laid and the compass of intention set, we embark on a voyage that promises to enlighten, empower, and transform. Let this book serve as your compass, guiding you through uncharted waters with the wisdom of the ages and the innovation of the modern world.

The Art of Money is not just a guide; it is an invitation to join a lineage of trailblazers, visionaries, and strategists who have harnessed the power of finance to shape their destinies. Let us embark upon this expedition together, for the voyage of financial mastery is one of profound significance—one that holds the potential to sculpt not only your own life but also the world at large.

Chapter 1: Foundations of Wealth Creation

The Mindset of Wealth

As we embark on our expedition into the world of wealth creation, it is paramount that we lay a strong bedrock upon which to build our financial edifice. This first sub-chapter, "The Mindset of Wealth," beckons us to delve beyond the realm of dollars and cents, urging us to explore the psychological landscape that underpins our financial journey. Buckle up, for we are about to traverse the labyrinth of beliefs, attitudes, and perspectives that shape our fiscal destiny.

Embracing an Abundance Mindset

Picture a garden. A garden nurtured with care, where seeds are sown, watered, and bathed in sunlight. The result? A vibrant tapestry of life, bursting forth with color, fragrance, and sustenance. Similarly, the garden of your financial life flourishes or withers based on the mindset you choose to cultivate.

An abundance mindset is the fertile soil from which financial success sprouts. It is an outlook that believes in the boundless opportunities that life presents. Instead of dwelling on scarcity, an abundance mindset acknowledges the universe's infinite capacity to provide. It shifts the focus from "I can't" to "How can I?" This shift in perspective becomes the catalyst for innovative ideas, ventures, and investments.

In the context of wealth creation, embracing an abundance mindset invites you to see beyond current limitations. It encourages you to view setbacks not as roadblocks but as stepping stones toward growth. An abundance mindset empowers you to recognize that wealth is not a finite resource, but a dynamic force waiting to be harnessed through strategic thinking and diligent action.

Overcoming Limiting Beliefs About Money
Our relationship with money often mirrors our deepest beliefs about ourselves. Unveiling these beliefs and challenging their accuracy can be a transformative step toward financial empowerment. Just as a sculptor chisels away at a block of marble to reveal the masterpiece within, so too must we chip away at our limiting beliefs to unveil our true potential.

Limiting beliefs often manifest as whispers that undermine our confidence and dampen our ambition. Thoughts like "I'm not good with money," "Rich people are greedy," or "I'll never be able to save enough" cast shadows over our financial aspirations. To conquer these limiting beliefs, we must shine the light of awareness upon them.

Start by questioning the origins of these beliefs. Are they based on personal experiences, societal conditioning, or inherited narratives? Then, challenge their validity. Seek evidence to counter these beliefs, whether through inspiring success stories, financial education, or your own achievements. Replace these disempowering beliefs with affirmations that align with your financial goals, slowly rewiring your mental framework.

Cultivating Patience and Long-Term Thinking
In a world of instant gratification, cultivating patience is akin to nurturing a rare and precious flower. Patience in wealth creation is not passive waiting; it is a deliberate, purposeful act of withstanding short-term impulses for the promise of greater rewards down the road.

Long-term thinking is the cornerstone of financial success. It involves stepping back from the immediacy of daily fluctuations and focusing on the bigger picture. Instead of seeking quick wins, long-term thinking encourages us to make decisions that compound over time, much like interest accruing on an investment.

Consider the story of the bamboo tree. When planted, it requires years of care and nurturing before it sprouts above the ground. But once it does, its growth is exponential, soaring to towering heights. Similarly, wealth creation often demands patience and persistence in the early stages, with rewards that blossom in due time.

Cultivating patience and long-term thinking involves mastering the art of delayed gratification. It means resisting the allure of impulse purchases and short-term gains in favor of enduring success. It involves aligning your actions with your long-term financial goals, even if it means making sacrifices in the present.

As we bid adieu to the realm of mindset, we emerge with a renewed perspective—an understanding that our thoughts and beliefs lay the foundation for our financial reality. An abundance mindset infuses our actions with creativity and courage, while the liberation from limiting beliefs empowers us to forge new narratives of financial success. Patience and long-term thinking equip us with the tools to navigate the twists and turns of our financial journey, transforming us into architects of our wealth.

Financial Literacy and Education

In our dynamic and interconnected world, the pursuit of wealth has transcended the boundaries of mere accumulation. It has evolved into an art form that requires an intricate blend of knowledge, strategy, and foresight. Welcome to the first sub-chapter of "The Art of Money," where we embark on a journey into the world of financial literacy and education—a journey that forms the bedrock of your mastery over wealth.

The Cornerstone: Understanding Basic Financial Concepts

Picture this: a building, towering and impressive, is constructed upon a solid foundation. In the realm of finance, that foundation is understanding basic financial concepts. This foundational knowledge is akin to the blueprint of your financial future. It encompasses an understanding of terms like income, expenses, assets, liabilities, and cash flow. Without a grasp of these fundamentals, the path to financial success remains elusive.

Every financial decision you make, whether it's choosing an investment avenue or managing debt, is predicated on these basics. The concept of budgeting, for instance, is not a mere exercise in tracking expenses; it's a way of aligning your spending with your financial aspirations. Think of it as a compass, guiding you toward the destination of financial security and abundance.

Learning About Vehicles and Strategies
Investing, often considered the artful dance between risk and reward, demands an in-depth understanding of investment vehicles and strategies. The landscape is rich and diverse, encompassing stocks, bonds, real estate, mutual funds, and the ever-evolving realm of cryptocurrencies. Each investment vehicle has its own characteristics, risk profiles, and potential for returns.

Delving into the world of investing is akin to becoming an astute collector. Just as an art connoisseur studies the nuances of different artists and genres, an informed investor studies the intricacies of different investment options. This involves grasping concepts such as compounding, diversification, and asset allocation. With knowledge as your guiding light, you can make informed decisions that align with your risk tolerance and financial goals.

However, remember that the art of investing extends beyond the technicalities. It also requires a keen sense of timing, a knack for spotting trends, and the wisdom to remain patient during market fluctuations. As we traverse this journey, you'll discover that the canvas of investment is a tapestry woven with insights from history, psychology, and the ever-changing global economy.

Embracing Evolution: Staying Updated with Economic Trends

In the landscape of finance, where change is constant, staying updated is paramount. Economic trends and market developments can shape your financial landscape in profound ways. Consider the rise of e-commerce and the subsequent shifts in retail. Think about the transformative impact of renewable energy on traditional energy industries. These shifts aren't just news headlines; they are pivotal events that influence investment opportunities and potential risks.

Being well-versed in economic trends involves keeping a watchful eye on global events, technological advancements, and shifts in consumer behavior. This isn't merely a spectator sport; it's an active engagement with the world around you. By anticipating changes and adapting your financial strategies accordingly, you position yourself as a participant rather than a bystander in the grand theater of finance.

Financial literacy and education serve as the cornerstone of your journey toward financial mastery. Just as an artist wields their brush with precision and intent, you too can wield your knowledge to shape your financial destiny. Understanding basic financial concepts, exploring investment vehicles and strategies, and staying attuned to economic trends are the hues you'll use to paint the masterpiece of your financial future.

As we journey onward through the chapters of "The Art of Money," remember that each step you take in your education is a brushstroke, each concept you grasp a stroke of genius. Stay curious, stay engaged, and stay committed to honing your skills. The road to financial empowerment begins with this very chapter—the chapter that empowers you with the tools to make informed decisions that will echo through your financial journey.

Setting Clear Financial Goals

Within the intricate tapestry of wealth creation, there exists a cornerstone that lays the foundation for all endeavors— clear and well-defined financial goals. In this sub chapter, we embark on a journey of introspection and strategic planning, unraveling the art of crafting objectives that transcend mere dreams and transform into reality.

**Defining Short-Term and Long-Term Financial
Objectives**

Imagine a ship without a course, a journey without a
destination. Our financial voyage is no different; without
well-defined goals, we drift aimlessly in a sea of
opportunities and distractions. To harness the power of
wealth creation, one must embark upon the path with
purpose and intent.

Short-term goals are the stepping stones to your larger
vision. These objectives, often spanning a year or less,
serve as benchmarks that keep you motivated and on track.
They might include paying off a credit card debt, saving for
a vacation, or building an emergency fund. Each
achievement contributes to your overall financial well-
being, bolstering your confidence and driving you forward.

Long-term goals, on the other hand, are the north stars that
guide your entire financial journey. These ambitions stretch
beyond the immediate horizon, often encompassing
milestones you wish to achieve in five, ten, twenty years, or
even longer. Examples of long-term goals could be
purchasing a home, funding your children's education,
achieving financial independence, or creating a legacy for
generations to come.

Creating a Roadmap for Achieving Your Goals

Goal setting is not merely about articulating your
aspirations—it's about crafting a roadmap that will lead you
to their realization. Imagine you're embarking on a cross-
country road trip; you'd meticulously plan your route,

ensuring you have the right resources, making necessary accommodations, and anticipating potential obstacles.

Similarly, your financial roadmap involves breaking down your goals into actionable steps. Begin by setting specific, measurable, achievable, relevant, and time-bound (SMART) objectives. For instance, if your long-term goal is to retire with a certain sum of money, you might break it down into smaller goals, such as contributing a specific amount to your retirement account annually.

Each goal should be accompanied by a set of tasks, deadlines, and checkpoints. This transforms your ambitions from abstract notions into a structured plan of action. It's the difference between saying, "I want to be financially secure" and "I will save 15% of my income every month and invest it in a diversified portfolio."

Monitoring Progress and Adjusting Goals as Needed
As you navigate your financial journey, the landscape will undoubtedly shift. Economic climates change, personal circumstances evolve, and unexpected opportunities or challenges may arise. This is why regular monitoring and flexibility are paramount in your pursuit of wealth creation.

Set regular intervals—monthly, quarterly, or annually—to assess your progress. Track your income, expenses, savings, investments, and net worth. Celebrate your achievements, and critically evaluate any setbacks or deviations from your plan. Adapting to changing circumstances doesn't signal failure; it demonstrates wisdom and pragmatism.

Should you encounter unforeseen challenges or seize unanticipated prospects, don't hesitate to adjust your goals accordingly. Flexibility is not a sign of wavering commitment; rather, it signifies your resilience in the face of a dynamic world. Your ability to pivot and realign your trajectory is a hallmark of a strategic and forward-thinking wealth creator.

Clear financial goals are the bedrock upon which your path to wealth creation is built. They serve as the guiding stars, illuminating your way through the intricate terrain of financial decisions. Defining short-term and long-term objectives, crafting a well-structured roadmap, and vigilantly monitoring your progress are the cornerstones of your journey.

Goal setting is not confined to paper and pen; it is a transformative process that empowers you to transcend limitations and take control of your financial destiny. In the chapters that follow, we will delve into the art of diversifying income streams, navigating economic challenges, and cultivating a mindset primed for success. Until then, may your ambitions be bold, your strategies meticulous, and your journey enlightening.

Chapter 2: Building Multiple Streams of Income

Diversifying Income Sources: A Pathway to Financial Fortitude

In the intricate tapestry of personal finance, the thread of income is perhaps the most vital strand. For centuries, the adage "don't put all your eggs in one basket" has echoed through the corridors of financial wisdom, urging individuals to embrace a multifaceted approach to income generation. Welcome to the realm of diversification—a cornerstone of financial prosperity that promises not only stability but also the potential for exponential growth.

The Landscape of Income Diversity

Imagine your income streams as a diversified portfolio, much like the investment strategies we explore in later chapters. The concept is elegant in its simplicity: instead of relying solely on one source of income, we open doors to a spectrum of opportunities. These opportunities span the terrain of employment, investments, and entrepreneurship.

At the heart of diversification lies the pursuit of resilience. A single income source, while providing security, can also render an individual susceptible to the unpredictable shifts of economic tides. By cultivating multiple streams of income, we fortify our financial foundation, creating a robust buffer against unexpected downturns.

The Triad of Income Sources

First in the triumvirate is the realm of employment—a cornerstone of financial stability for many. The dependable paycheck brings with it a sense of security, ensuring regularity in meeting essential needs. However, the confines of a single job can sometimes limit our earning potential. It's essential to explore avenues that enhance your career trajectory, ensuring a trajectory that aligns with both your passions and the market's demands.

Next, we venture into the realm of investments—an art form that transcends mere financial transactions. Investments breathe life into your money, transforming it into a catalyst for growth. Stocks, bonds, real estate, and mutual funds, to name a few, offer gateways to passive income. These investments serve as tendrils that reach into the soil of opportunity, sowing seeds that, over time, blossom into financial abundance.

Finally, the third facet—entrepreneurship—holds the allure of autonomy and limitless potential. Entrepreneurs are modern-day alchemists, transmuting ideas into enterprises. This journey is not without its challenges, but for those willing to embrace risk and innovation, entrepreneurship offers an avenue to unlimited income streams. The entrepreneur harnesses the power of creativity and strategy, crafting value in exchange for financial reward.

Balancing Act: Active and Passive Income

Within the realm of diversification lies the delicate equilibrium between active and passive income. Active income, often associated with employment and entrepreneurship, demands your direct involvement. It's the sweat equity—the hours, energy, and expertise invested. Passive income, on the other hand, manifests as the proverbial "money working for you." Investments and assets generate income without the constant demand for active engagement.

While active income provides immediate gratification, passive income extends the promise of financial independence. The beauty of diversification lies in its ability to balance these two forces. By cultivating both active and passive streams, you create a financial symphony where the crescendo of your efforts yields both immediate rewards and the promise of long-term wealth.

Diversifying your income sources is a testament to your adaptability and foresight. It's a commitment to a multifaceted journey where each income stream harmonizes with the others, contributing to a symphony of financial well-being. A symphony that plays not only for you but for generations to come.

Entrepreneurial Ventures

In the symphony of wealth-building, one of the most harmonious notes is struck by the pursuit of entrepreneurial ventures. The allure of charting your own course, crafting a unique value proposition, and reaping the rewards of your ingenuity has drawn countless individuals into the realm of entrepreneurship. In this sub-chapter, we delve into the art of identifying promising business opportunities, constructing a robust business plan, and orchestrating the crescendo of scaling for amplified income.

Identifying Business Opportunities Aligned with Your Strengths

Entrepreneurship is more than a mere transaction; it's a dance between your passion, your talents, and the needs of the market. To embark on a successful entrepreneurial journey, begin by reflecting on your strengths, skills, and areas of expertise. The magic happens when you meld these attributes with a gap in the market—a need that remains unmet or underserved.

Consider the stories of those who have walked this path before. They have transformed their hobbies into thriving enterprises, their insights into disruptive innovations, and their expertise into solutions that improve lives. Your unique perspective and capabilities can be your compass in navigating the sea of possibilities. Listen to your intuition, observe market trends, and seek alignment between your passions and the needs of the world.

Developing a Business Plan and Value Proposition

Entrepreneurship is not a leap into the unknown; it's a journey guided by a well-crafted roadmap—the business plan. This document is more than a formality; it's a blueprint that outlines your business's purpose, target market, value proposition, revenue model, and growth strategies. A robust business plan serves as your North Star, guiding your decisions and offering a structured approach to realizing your entrepreneurial vision.

Central to your business plan is the value proposition—the soul of your venture. It's the answer to the question: "Why should customers choose your product or service over others?" A compelling value proposition resonates with your target audience, addressing their pain points and showcasing the unique benefits your offering brings. Remember, a strong value proposition isn't just about what you offer, but how it enhances the lives of your customers.

Scaling and Expanding Your Ventures for Increased Income

As your entrepreneurial venture gains traction, the prospect of scaling presents itself—a transformative phase that requires careful orchestration. Scaling isn't just about increasing revenue; it's about replicating and amplifying your success while maintaining the essence of what made your venture special in the first place.

Scaling demands strategic thinking, resource allocation, and a keen understanding of market dynamics. It's about expanding your reach, diversifying your customer base, and exploring new avenues for growth. Yet, with growth comes complexity, and your ability to manage this complexity while retaining the essence of your business's value proposition will determine your longevity.

Consider the stories of companies that have scaled elegantly. They've embraced innovation, leveraged technology, and fostered a culture that thrives on adaptability. Scaling is not a monolithic endeavor; it's a series of calculated steps, punctuated by iterative learning and an unwavering commitment to delivering value.

In this era of unprecedented connectivity, technology provides an array of tools for scaling, from digital marketing and e-commerce platforms to data analytics that uncover customer insights. Your ability to harness these tools will be pivotal in the journey from entrepreneurial venture to an impactful, enduring enterprise.

Entrepreneurial ventures embody the spirit of innovation, tenacity, and value creation. From identifying opportunities to developing a robust business plan and scaling for growth, this sub-chapter unveils the intricate steps that pave the way for income amplification. Entrepreneurship is a canvas where your creativity, expertise, and determination can converge to paint a masterpiece of success. As you embark on this voyage, let your strengths illuminate the path, your vision guide the ship, and your commitment fuel the journey towards entrepreneurial triumph.

Investment Strategies

In the labyrinth of financial possibilities, where dreams of wealth are shaped into tangible reality, investment strategies emerge as the cornerstone of sustainable prosperity. This sub-chapter is an invitation to unravel the intricate dance between risk and reward, to explore the myriad avenues through which your hard-earned capital can be nurtured to flourish.

Understanding Risk and Reward in Investment

Picture a tightrope walker poised above a bustling cityscape. With each step, they are driven by a delicate balance: the thrill of progress versus the fear of a fall. Similarly, the world of investments dances on this tightrope, where potential rewards beckon from one side, and the lurking shadow of risk hovers on the other.

Understanding risk and reward is not merely an intellectual pursuit—it's a fundamental mindset that shapes your approach to investment. Every investment avenue comes with its own risk profile, and the art lies in aligning your risk tolerance with the potential gains. Stocks may offer higher returns, but they also bear the volatility of market fluctuations. Bonds, on the other hand, are known for stability but might provide more modest returns.

Yet, risk is not inherently negative; it's the bedrock of opportunity. In the realm of investments, risk and reward are inextricably linked. To navigate this duality, it's crucial to assess your own risk appetite, financial goals, and time horizon. Are you aiming for short-term gains or long-term growth? How much volatility can you stomach? Armed with these insights, you can chart a course that balances the allure of reward with the prudence of risk management.

Exploring Investment Options: Stocks, Real Estate, Bonds, and Beyond

Investment strategies present an array of choices akin to a gourmet buffet, each option offering a distinct flavor of potential returns. Among these options, stocks, real estate, and bonds stand as pillars of financial growth, each with its unique characteristics and implications.

Stocks: A slice of ownership in a company, stocks offer the allure of high returns, often outpacing inflation over the long run. However, the stock market is characterized by its volatility, influenced by factors ranging from macroeconomic trends to corporate performance. Investing in stocks demands careful research and a willingness to weather market fluctuations.

Real Estate: Often referred to as the "tangible asset," real estate investment provides both rental income and potential appreciation. The stability of property investment can serve as a hedge against market volatility. Nonetheless, real estate entails costs such as property management, maintenance, and the potential for vacancy periods.

Bonds: Bonds are debt securities issued by governments and corporations. They offer fixed interest payments and serve as a relatively stable investment option. Bonds can be particularly appealing for risk-averse investors seeking consistent income. However, it's important to note that bond prices can be influenced by interest rate changes.

Venturing beyond these foundational options, the investment landscape has expanded to embrace alternative assets such as commodities, cryptocurrencies, and exchange-traded funds (ETFs). Each of these avenues brings its own set of considerations, risk factors, and potential rewards.

Creating a Diversified Investment Portfolio: The Power of Balance

Imagine a symphony—a harmonious arrangement of diverse instruments, each contributing to the grandeur of the composition. Similarly, a diversified investment portfolio orchestrates a balance of assets that can weather storms and seize opportunities across different market conditions.

Diversification is the practice of spreading investments across various asset classes, sectors, and geographies. This strategy reduces the impact of a single investment's poor performance on the overall portfolio. By holding a mix of assets with varying risk profiles, you can aim to capture growth while mitigating potential losses.

Creating a diversified portfolio requires a careful blend of research, analysis, and adaptability. A well-balanced portfolio considers your risk tolerance, financial goals, and investment horizon. It might include a combination of stocks, bonds, real estate, and perhaps alternative investments. Regular monitoring and rebalancing ensure that the portfolio maintains its intended allocation.

In this age of digital connectivity, technology has democratized investment strategies, offering tools and platforms that empower individuals to build their portfolios with ease. Robo-advisors and online brokerage accounts provide access to diversified portfolios tailored to your preferences and risk profile.

Investment strategies weave the fabric of your financial future. They embody your aspirations, your risk tolerance, and your belief in the power of compound growth. As you navigate the world of investments, remember that every choice you make is a brushstroke on the canvas of your financial destiny.

The dance between risk and reward is not a sprint; it's a rhythmic journey. As you explore the multifaceted realm of stocks, real estate, bonds, and more, bear in mind that investment success is rarely instant. It's the result of informed decisions, patient endurance, and a willingness to adapt.

Chapter 3: Smart Spending and Budgeting

Creating a Sustainable Budget

In the vast tapestry of wealth management, few threads are as essential as the art of budgeting. It is the cornerstone upon which financial empires are built, the compass that guides us through the labyrinth of expenses and income. As we embark on this sub-chapter, we delve into the realm of "Creating a Sustainable Budget," where every dollar becomes a brushstroke, carefully applied to craft a masterpiece of financial stability.

Tracking Expenses and Income: Illuminating the Financial Landscape

Before you can take the reins of your financial destiny, you must first understand the lay of the land. Just as a cartographer charts unexplored territories, you must chart the realm of your expenses and income. Tracking these financial currents reveals patterns that would otherwise remain concealed.

Begin by meticulously documenting every expenditure. Whether it's the morning latte, the monthly rent, or the occasional indulgence, nothing is too insignificant to record. Modern technology has bestowed upon us an array of tools—apps, spreadsheets, and software—that can transform this often-daunting task into a streamlined process. With every entry, you unveil a panorama of your financial behavior.

Income, too, demands a watchful eye. Regular paychecks, freelance earnings, or investment returns—all sources of revenue should be diligently recorded. This comprehensive record illuminates the peaks and valleys of your financial landscape, fostering an understanding that is pivotal to crafting an effective budget.

Allocating Funds: The Orchestra of Priorities
Imagine your finances as an orchestra, with each instrument representing a facet of your financial life. A sustainable budget directs the symphony, ensuring every note is harmonious and contributes to the grand composition. Essential expenses—the strings that provide structure—are allocated their share first. These include housing, utilities, groceries, transportation, and other necessities.

Once the essential strings resonate, it's time to let the wind instruments of savings and investments weave their melodies. Set a portion of your income aside for the future, allowing compound interest to transform a modest contribution into a formidable force. Treat these allocations as non-negotiable, paying yourself first to build a robust financial foundation.

But no masterpiece is complete without a sprinkle of color, a dash of spontaneity. Thus, the woodwinds of leisure and discretionary spending emerge. Budgeting doesn't demand austerity; it advocates balance. Set aside a portion for entertainment, dining out, and the occasional indulgence.

This not only prevents burnout but also infuses joy into the journey of financial management.

Avoiding Unnecessary Expenditures: The Art of Discernment

In the bazaar of modern living, temptations and distractions abound. From flashy gadgets to fleeting trends, the siren call of unnecessary expenditures can divert even the most disciplined of budgeters. The key to resisting these temptations lies in cultivating discernment.

Before every purchase, pause and reflect. Does this align with your financial goals? Will it bring enduring value or provide momentary gratification? By evaluating each expense through the lens of its contribution to your larger financial tapestry, you can shield yourself from impulsive spending.

Additionally, consider the concept of the "latte factor." Small daily expenses, like that morning coffee, might seem trivial in isolation, but cumulatively, they can erode your budget. Identifying and curbing these micro-expenditures can free up funds for more meaningful pursuits.

Crafting a sustainable budget is not a rigid process, but rather a fluid symphony that evolves with your life. As your income, expenses, and priorities shift, so too must your budget adapt. Regularly revisit and fine-tune your budget, ensuring it remains aligned with your financial aspirations.

This sub-chapter, "Creating a Sustainable Budget," serves as the blueprint for financial harmony. It urges you to engage with your finances mindfully, recognizing that every allocation is a brushstroke contributing to your financial masterpiece. Let your budget become a reflection of your values, priorities, and aspirations—an orchestration that guides you towards prosperity and security.

With every expense tracked, every allocation made, and every unnecessary expenditure averted, you move closer to the pinnacle of financial mastery. As the conductor of your financial orchestra, you wield the baton of awareness and strategy, ensuring that your finances resonate with purpose, balance, and resonance.

Effective Cost Management

In the intricate dance of wealth management, where every dollar holds the potential to shape your financial destiny, mastering the art of cost management is akin to conducting a symphony of frugality and discernment. Here, we delve into the essential practices that separate the prudent financial navigator from the heedless spender. Effective cost management transcends mere penny-pinching; it's a strategic approach that empowers you to optimize your resources, minimize wasteful expenditures, and amplify your capacity to grow and safeguard your wealth.

Differentiating Between Needs and Wants
In a world constantly enticing us with the allure of convenience, luxury, and the latest trends, the line between needs and wants can blur into obscurity. Effective cost management requires you to reclaim this line and draw it with precision. Needs are the essentials, the fundamental components that sustain your life, well-being, and ability to function optimally. Wants, on the other hand, are the embellishments that might enrich your experience but are not indispensable.

Understanding this distinction empowers you to allocate your resources with wisdom. Ask yourself: "Is this a necessity that directly contributes to my well-being and goals, or is it a fleeting desire that might provide short-term pleasure but detract from my long-term financial security?" Practicing this discernment can curb impulsive spending and align your expenditures with your overarching financial strategy.

Negotiating Deals and Seeking Value for Money
In a world where almost everything is negotiable, from your monthly bills to larger purchases, the art of negotiation becomes a formidable tool in your cost management arsenal. The act of negotiating isn't about mere haggling; it's a strategic dance that requires research, preparation, and the ability to convey value.

Before entering negotiations, arm yourself with knowledge about the product or service, comparable market prices, and potential incentives. Approach the negotiation with confidence and respect, highlighting the value you bring as a customer. Remember, successful negotiation isn't solely about driving the price down; it's about achieving a win-win scenario where both parties feel satisfied with the outcome.

Furthermore, seeking value for your money doesn't stop at negotiations. It extends to scrutinizing the quality, durability, and long-term benefits of what you're purchasing. A product with a slightly higher upfront cost but superior quality might prove more cost-effective over its lifespan compared to a cheaper alternative that requires frequent replacement.

Using Technology and Tools for Expense Tracking
In an era defined by technological innovation, harnessing the power of digital tools and apps can revolutionize your approach to expense tracking. Gone are the days of manually jotting down expenditures in a ledger; modern technology provides a plethora of user-friendly platforms that allow you to monitor your finances with ease.

Expense tracking apps enable you to categorize your spending, set budgets, and receive alerts when you approach predefined limits. By visualizing your spending patterns, you gain insights into where your money is flowing and identify areas where you can cut back or optimize.

Beyond apps, credit card and bank statements, and receipts can offer a wealth of data. Analyzing these records can

reveal spending habits you might not have been conscious
of, helping you make informed adjustments. Effective
expense tracking is not about restricting your freedom, but
about empowering you to make informed choices aligned
with your financial goals.

Effective cost management isn't a practice of deprivation,
but rather one of empowerment. It grants you the ability to
make conscious choices, channeling your financial
resources toward endeavors that truly matter. By
distinguishing between needs and wants, harnessing the art
of negotiation, and embracing technology for expense
tracking, you're poised to embark on a journey of
heightened financial consciousness and strategic resource
allocation. Remember, every dollar saved today has the
potential to multiply its impact in your future wealth
landscape.

Managing Debt Wisely

In the intricate tapestry of financial wellness, the threads of
debt form a significant motif. While the notion of debt
might conjure up negative connotations, it's crucial to
understand that not all debt is created equal. In this sub-
chapter, we delve into the delicate art of managing debt
wisely—a skill that can make the difference between a
burden and a stepping stone towards prosperity.

Understanding Good Debt vs. Bad Debt

Before we embark on the journey of managing debt, let's address the distinction between good debt and bad debt. Good debt, contrary to what the name might suggest, can actually be an asset in your financial arsenal. It's debt incurred for investments that have the potential to increase in value or generate income over time. For instance, taking out a mortgage to purchase a home or financing your education can fall into the category of good debt. These investments have the potential to yield long-term returns that outweigh the initial borrowing costs.

On the flip side, bad debt encompasses liabilities incurred for purchases that depreciate in value or offer no lasting benefits. High-interest credit card debt, payday loans, and financing consumer goods that rapidly lose value are prime examples of bad debt. These financial commitments can quickly spiral into burdens that stifle your financial growth.

Developing a Plan for Paying Off Debts

If you find yourself entangled in the web of debt, take solace in the fact that there's a way out—a path illuminated by strategic planning and disciplined execution. The first step towards debt liberation involves developing a comprehensive debt repayment plan.

Begin by listing all your outstanding debts, including credit card balances, student loans, car loans, and any other liabilities. Assign each debt a priority based on factors such as interest rates, due dates, and overall balances. Once you've established a hierarchy, consider two primary approaches for repayment: the "Snowball" method and the "Avalanche" method.

The Snowball method involves directing extra payments towards the smallest debt while making minimum payments on other obligations. As you eliminate smaller debts, you gain a sense of accomplishment and motivation to tackle larger ones. The Avalanche method, on the other hand, targets debts with the highest interest rates first, mathematically optimizing your repayments to reduce overall interest costs.

Whichever method you choose, consistency and dedication are paramount. Allocate a portion of your budget towards debt repayment each month, and as you witness your balances decrease, you'll experience not only financial relief but also a surge in confidence.

Avoiding High-Interest Debt Traps
In the labyrinth of debt management, one treacherous path is paved with high-interest debt traps. These financial instruments might promise quick cash or easy purchases, but their hidden costs can wreak havoc on your financial stability. Payday loans, for instance, come with exorbitant interest rates that can lead borrowers into a cycle of perpetual indebtedness. Similarly, high-interest credit cards can transform a small balance into a mountain of debt if not managed prudently.

To avoid these pitfalls, cultivate an acute awareness of the terms and conditions of any borrowing you consider.

Scrutinize interest rates, repayment schedules, and potential hidden fees. Prioritize financial institutions known for transparency and ethical lending practices. As a rule of thumb, if an offer seems too good to be true, it probably is. Seek alternatives, such as negotiating with creditors or exploring community resources for financial assistance, before resorting to high-interest loans.

The realm of debt is a complex landscape that demands respect and strategic navigation. Understanding the nuances of good and bad debt, formulating a meticulous repayment plan, and evading high-interest debt traps are essential steps towards mastering this aspect of your financial journey. As you untangle the threads of indebtedness, you carve a path towards financial freedom—one that liberates you to invest in your future, unburdened by the weight of unsustainable liabilities.

Chapter 4: Strategic Investments

Value Investing

In the bustling arena of finance, where trends shift like sand dunes and opportunities seem to flicker like distant stars, a steady and time-tested strategy known as "Value Investing" stands as a lighthouse amidst the tumultuous sea of speculation. As we venture into the realm of strategic investments, we delve into the first sub-chapter, "Value Investing," an art form that embodies the essence of rationality, thorough analysis, and patience in the pursuit of financial growth.

Researching Undervalued Assets: The Quest for Hidden Potential

Value investing commences with a mindset akin to that of a seasoned explorer setting forth on a quest for hidden treasures. The core tenet here is to seek out assets that the market has unjustly undervalued. Such undervaluation could stem from temporary market sentiment, overlooked opportunities, or a lack of thorough analysis by the investing crowd.

To embark on this journey, one must equip themselves with the tools of research and analysis. This involves meticulous scrutiny of industries, companies, and market trends. Armed with a curious mind and a discerning eye, value investors aim to uncover the proverbial "diamonds in the rough." This process requires a combination of fundamental analysis, technical assessment, and an intuitive understanding of economic forces at play.

Analyzing Fundamentals and Financial Statements: The Art of Evaluation

At the heart of value investing lies the art of evaluating the fundamentals. Financial statements—balance sheets, income statements, and cash flow statements—reveal the intricate dance of a company's revenues, expenses, assets, and liabilities. These documents are not merely columns of numbers; they are windows into the health and potential of a business.

Value investors pore over financial statements with a meticulous eye, searching for discrepancies between the perceived value of a company and its market price. This analysis, coupled with a thorough understanding of industry dynamics and market competition, guides the selection process. Moreover, a value investor considers factors such as a company's competitive advantage, growth prospects, and management quality, all of which play a crucial role in determining its intrinsic value.

Patience as a Key Value Investing Principle: The Virtue of Time

The virtue of patience has often been proclaimed a cornerstone of successful investing, and value investing exemplifies this principle beautifully. In a world driven by instantaneous news cycles and rapid-fire trading, value investing stands as a beacon of stability. Value investors understand that the market's whims can create temporary dissonance between a company's intrinsic value and its market price.

Patience, in this context, does not imply passivity; it signifies an unwavering commitment to the long-term vision. Value investors are willing to wait for the market to correct its misjudgments, aligning the stock's price with its true worth. This patient approach allows for the compounding effects of time to work their magic, transforming undervalued assets into profitable investments.

The likes of Warren Buffett and Benjamin Graham, revered luminaries in the field of finance, have demonstrated the power of patience and value-based investing. Their portfolios have showcased the remarkable growth that can be achieved by resisting the allure of quick gains in favor of steady, calculated strategies.

Value investing is not a mere formula; it is an art that marries analytical rigor with a profound appreciation for the true worth of investments. As we venture forth into the world of strategic investments, remember that value investing is not a sprint, but a marathon—a journey that rewards those who are willing to uncover hidden treasures, decipher financial melodies, and savor the sweet symphony of long-term financial prosperity.

Real Estate Opportunities

In the tapestry of investment opportunities, few threads are as enduring and transformative as real estate. The allure of owning tangible assets, the potential for passive income, and the promise of capital appreciation have drawn countless investors into the realm of property investment. Within this realm lies a universe of possibilities, where shrewd strategies and a deep understanding of the market can turn bricks and mortar into a fortress of wealth.

Diversification, often touted as a cardinal rule of investing, finds a worthy ally in real estate. Amid the whirlwind of stock market volatility and the capriciousness of financial instruments, real estate offers a bastion of stability. While the allure of stocks and bonds remains undeniable, the tangible nature of real estate imparts a sense of security that is difficult to replicate in the digital realm.

Exploring Rental Properties and Real Estate Development

One of the fundamental avenues in real estate investment lies in rental properties. The concept is elegantly simple: acquire a property, secure a tenant, and generate a steady stream of income. Yet, beneath this simplicity lies a labyrinth of considerations that demand your attention. From choosing the right location to understanding local rental market dynamics, every decision is a brushstroke on the canvas of your investment portfolio.

The value of rental properties extends beyond their monetary returns. With each lease signed, you become part of a community, serving as a custodian of living spaces for individuals and families. However, this endeavor is not without its challenges. Tenants, maintenance, and property management require meticulous attention to detail. In the world of real estate investment, being a landlord entails not only financial acumen but also a commitment to creating a positive living experience.

But the realm of real estate is not solely about passive income through rental properties; it's also about the creative journey of real estate development. This path involves taking raw land or existing properties and shaping them into valuable assets. Real estate development necessitates a blend of vision, strategic planning, and execution prowess. From residential complexes to commercial spaces, each project has the potential to reshape skylines and communities, while simultaneously enriching your investment portfolio.

Understanding Property Market Cycles
While the siren call of real estate investment is strong, it's important to recognize that the property market is not immune to cycles. Just as financial markets experience bull and bear phases, property markets follow their own patterns of expansion and contraction. The ability to identify and interpret these cycles is a skill that separates the savvy investor from the impulsive buyer.

The market cycle is a dance of supply, demand, interest rates, economic health, and geopolitical factors. A comprehensive understanding of these elements empowers you to make informed decisions about when to enter or exit the market. The timing of your investment can significantly impact its potential returns. It's essential to avoid chasing fleeting trends and instead, base your decisions on a solid grasp of market fundamentals.

Managing Real Estate Investments Effectively
Effectively managing real estate investments extends beyond the initial purchase. Just as a finely tuned orchestra requires a conductor, your investment portfolio requires vigilant oversight. This includes optimizing rental income, ensuring regular maintenance, and being prepared to adapt to market shifts.

Property management, whether undertaken independently or through professional services, demands organization, communication, and responsiveness. Addressing tenant concerns promptly, conducting regular property inspections, and keeping a vigilant eye on market trends are all part of the orchestra that creates harmony within your real estate portfolio.

The realm of real estate is one of endless possibilities and challenges. The journey from exploring rental properties and real estate development to understanding market cycles and effective management is a multifaceted one. It's a journey that requires not only a keen understanding of financial dynamics but also a heart for creating spaces and communities. As you tread this path, remember that every brick laid and every lease signed contributes not only to your own financial well-being but also to the intricate tapestry of a thriving society.

Alternative Investments: Navigating Uncharted Territories

In the ever-evolving landscape of finance, where traditional avenues often teem with competition and conformity, alternative investments emerge as the enigmatic outliers—a realm where commodities, cryptocurrencies, and precious metals weave a tapestry of intrigue and opportunity. This sub-chapter is your portal into this captivating domain, an exploration of uncharted territories that beckon the daring investor with promises of unique risks and rewards.

Conventional investment vehicles such as stocks and bonds form the cornerstone of most portfolios, but savvy investors understand that venturing beyond these customary territories can offer a spectrum of benefits. Alternative investments, while often characterized by higher complexity and risk, possess a distinct allure due to their potential to hedge against market volatility and generate non-correlated returns.

Commodities: From the Earth to the Market

Commodities, the raw materials that fuel industries and economies, offer a gateway to investing in the tangible essence of production. From precious metals like gold and silver to energy sources like oil and natural gas, commodities provide a tangible link between economic demand and supply. Investing in commodities can be both speculative and practical, driven by factors ranging from geopolitical tensions to global supply chain disruptions.

Understanding the cyclical nature of commodity markets is paramount. The ebb and flow of demand, influenced by global economic trends, technological advancements, and shifts in consumer behavior, can significantly impact prices. As such, astute investors analyze supply-demand dynamics, geopolitical events, and macroeconomic trends to navigate the intricate landscape of commodities.

Cryptocurrencies: The Digital Frontier
Cryptocurrencies, born from the convergence of technology and finance, have rapidly transformed from mere technological curiosities to legitimate investment assets. While the concept of digital currencies may evoke a futuristic aura, the underlying technologies—most notably, blockchain—have disrupted traditional financial paradigms.

Bitcoin, often hailed as digital gold, opened the door to a myriad of cryptocurrencies each with their own unique features and utilities. The decentralized nature of cryptocurrencies, coupled with potential for significant price volatility, presents both opportunities and challenges. Investors venturing into this realm should undertake comprehensive research, delving into the intricacies of blockchain technology, understanding the utility of specific coins, and staying attuned to regulatory developments.

Precious Metals: Guardians of Value

In times of economic uncertainty, precious metals have historically retained their allure as "safe-haven" assets. Gold and silver, in particular, have long been revered not only for their aesthetic appeal but also for their capacity to preserve wealth. Precious metals shine brightest when financial markets experience turbulence or when inflation threatens the purchasing power of traditional currencies.

The appeal of precious metals extends beyond mere investment; they can also serve as a hedge against currency depreciation and geopolitical instability. Physical ownership of precious metals, whether in the form of coins, bars, or bullion, offers a tangible connection to enduring value. However, it's essential to acknowledge that while precious metals may hold their value, they do not generate income like dividends from stocks or interest from bonds.

Integrating alternative investments into a diversified portfolio

The allure of alternative investments lies not only in their individual potential but also in their capacity to complement and diversify traditional investment holdings. Integrating commodities, cryptocurrencies, or precious metals into a diversified portfolio can help mitigate risk and enhance overall returns. The key lies in striking a delicate balance between conventional and alternative assets, aligning your investment choices with your risk tolerance, investment horizon, and financial goals.

As you embark on your journey into the realm of alternative investments, remember that knowledge is your compass. The intricate landscapes of commodities, cryptocurrencies, and precious metals demand a thorough understanding of market dynamics, technological underpinnings, and regulatory influences. While the potential rewards can be substantial, so too are the risks. Approach this realm with a blend of caution and curiosity, and may your journey be one of both exploration and enlightenment.

Chapter 5: Risk Management and Preservation

Importance of Risk Assessment

In the grand tapestry of wealth creation and preservation, the warp and weft of risk management form the intricate pattern that holds it all together. As we delve into the realm of risk assessment, we unveil a critical facet of financial mastery—one that distinguishes the unprepared from the prudent, the resilient from the vulnerable. Brace yourself for a journey into the heart of uncertainty, where we dissect vulnerabilities, fortify defenses, and emerge empowered to navigate the capricious seas of finance.

Identifying Financial Vulnerabilities and Potential Risks

In the realms of finance, where fortunes are built and futures secured, it is imperative to face the shadows without fear. This is the essence of risk assessment: the art of unveiling vulnerabilities lurking beneath the surface and illuminating them with the torch of foresight.

Vulnerabilities come in various forms—economic downturns, unforeseen health crises, job loss, and unexpected liabilities. To uncover them requires an unflinching evaluation of our financial landscape. Begin by scrutinizing your income streams, liabilities, and expenditures. Understand the intricacies of your financial ecosystem, from investments and debts to insurance coverage and savings.

This process requires a candid assessment of your risk tolerance. Are you comfortable navigating tumultuous markets, or do you lean towards conservative investments? Recognizing your emotional response to risk is an invaluable first step in understanding the challenges you're willing to embrace and those you'd rather avoid.

Mitigating Risks Through Insurance and Emergency Funds

In a world where the unforeseen often takes center stage, insurance emerges as a potent shield against financial devastation. It is a mechanism by which we transfer risk to entities equipped to bear it. Homeowners' insurance, health insurance, and life insurance—all these safeguard against scenarios that could otherwise derail even the most meticulously laid financial plans.

However, it's essential to approach insurance with discernment. Assess the coverage you truly require and avoid overextending yourself. Collaborate with insurance professionals who can help tailor your coverage to your unique circumstances, ensuring you're neither underinsured nor overinsured.

But insurance is only one layer of the protective armor. In the arsenal of risk management, the emergency fund stands as a cornerstone. It's a reservoir of liquidity—a buffer that shields against the unforeseen. This fund should be sufficient to cover three to six months' worth of living expenses. Should a sudden job loss or medical emergency arise, your emergency fund offers the financial breathing room required to navigate the turbulence with equanimity.

Preparing for Unexpected Life Events
Life is a journey paved with twists and turns, and the road isn't always smooth. Unexpected life events—such as medical emergencies, accidents, or sudden career changes—can exert unforeseen pressures on your financial stability. To navigate these upheavals effectively, foresight and planning are your trusted companions.

One powerful tool in this arsenal is a comprehensive estate plan. Estate planning encompasses everything from wills and trusts to powers of attorney and advance healthcare directives. It ensures your wishes are honored and your assets are distributed as you envision, reducing potential disputes and legal complications during times of distress.

Moreover, it's prudent to maintain open lines of communication with family members or dependents who could be affected by your financial decisions. Discuss your plans and intentions openly, so everyone is on the same page, prepared to handle any potential changes.

The process of risk assessment isn't about eliminating risk entirely—that's an impossibility in the realm of finance. Rather, it's about understanding, quantifying, and mitigating risk to the best of your ability. By embracing risk assessment, you acknowledge the uncertainties that life inevitably presents, and in doing so, you empower yourself to tread confidently on the path to financial mastery.

Estate Planning and Wealth Transfer

In the vast expanse of the financial landscape, there exists a facet that often stands overshadowed by the pursuit of profits and growth—the meticulous craft of estate planning. Just as an architect drafts blueprints to construct a sturdy building, and an artist layers pigments to form a masterpiece, estate planning involves the art of sculpting a legacy that extends beyond one's earthly journey. In this sub-chapter, we delve into the intricacies of estate planning and the seamless transfer of wealth—a vital cornerstone in the edifice of financial mastery.

Crafting a Comprehensive Estate Plan

Imagine your estate plan as a treasure map, a meticulously charted guide that ensures your wealth is distributed according to your wishes while minimizing potential disruptions for your loved ones. Your estate plan, like the masterstroke of a painter's brush, is a reflection of your values, desires, and dreams. It is a testament to your dedication not only to accumulating wealth but also to preserving its impact through generations.

Creating a comprehensive estate plan involves several crucial components:

1. Will and Testament: A Beacon of Intent

The foundation of any estate plan is the will—a document that outlines how you wish your assets to be distributed upon your passing. It serves as a beacon of intent, illuminating your desires for your loved ones and ensuring that your assets find their rightful places. Beyond the distribution of wealth, a will allows you to designate guardians for minor children, specify funeral arrangements, and even express your values to future generations.

2. Trusts: The Guardians of Legacy

Trusts are akin to the frames that safeguard a prized artwork. They can be designed to manage and distribute assets while offering benefits such as reducing estate taxes and avoiding probate. Irrevocable trusts can provide an avenue to separate assets from your estate, minimizing potential tax liabilities. Revocable living trusts, on the other hand, allow you to maintain control over your assets during your lifetime while ensuring seamless wealth transfer after your passing.

3. Powers of Attorney and Healthcare Directives: Ensuring Continuity

In the realm of estate planning, it's not only the monetary assets that demand attention; your well-being and wishes also hold paramount importance. Designating powers of attorney and drafting healthcare directives empowers trusted individuals to make financial and medical decisions on your behalf should you become incapacitated. This ensures the continuity of your financial affairs and the implementation of your healthcare choices.

Minimizing Estate Taxes and Legal Complexities
The symphony of wealth transfer carries with it a distinct note—the potential for estate taxes. Navigating these tax waters requires a skilled conductor who can harmonize the legacy you desire with the legal intricacies involved. One key strategy in this endeavor is understanding the estate tax threshold. By comprehending the thresholds, you can structure your estate plan to minimize tax liabilities and maximize the inheritance passed on to your heirs.

1. Gifting Strategies: The Art of Generosity

Strategic gifting during your lifetime can serve both philanthropic and financial objectives. Gifting can reduce the taxable value of your estate while enabling you to witness the impact of your generosity. Utilizing annual gift exclusions and lifetime gift exemptions, you can transfer assets to loved ones with minimal tax consequences.

2. Charitable Giving: Weaving Social Impact

In the symphony of wealth transfer, the notes of philanthropy resonate with a resonance that transcends generations. Charitable giving not only supports causes close to your heart but can also significantly reduce estate tax liabilities. Establishing charitable remainder trusts or charitable lead trusts can offer a win-win scenario—supporting a cause while minimizing the burden of estate taxes on your heirs.

Ensuring a Smooth Wealth Transition for Future Generations

As you embark on the journey of estate planning, remember that your efforts extend far beyond your lifetime. Ensuring a seamless wealth transition for future generations requires not only the technical finesse of legal structures but also the wisdom to nurture financial education and responsible stewardship.

1. Family Meetings and Communication: Passing the Torch of Wisdom

Open and transparent communication about your estate plan can dispel potential conflicts and misunderstandings among your heirs. Hosting family meetings to discuss the intentions and reasoning behind your decisions provides your loved ones with clarity, helping to forge a united front when the time comes for wealth transition.

2. Education and Financial Literacy: Empowering Heirs

Passing on your wealth is not merely about bequeathing assets; it's about imparting the knowledge and skills necessary to navigate the responsibilities that accompany it. Fostering financial literacy and providing education to your heirs equips them to make informed decisions, ensuring that the legacy you've built is not just preserved but elevated.

3. Professional Guidance: Orchestrating the Transition

Amid the intricacies of estate planning, professional guidance is an invaluable asset. Enlisting the expertise of estate attorneys, financial planners, and tax advisors can illuminate potential pitfalls and guide you toward the most effective strategies for preserving wealth and easing its transfer.

Estate planning emerges as an art form—one that requires meticulous attention, thoughtful consideration, and a deep appreciation for the legacy you wish to leave. As you navigate this chapter of your financial journey, remember that estate planning is not just about the preservation of assets; it's about the preservation of values, dreams, and impact that echo through time.

Long-Term Wealth Preservation

The art of preserving what has been diligently amassed stands as a pivotal masterpiece to personal wealth management. As we delve into the intricate realm of long-term wealth preservation, our focus shifts from the vigor of accumulation to the wisdom of safeguarding. This sub-chapter will be your compass, guiding you through the intricate landscape of balancing growth with preservation, the strategic adaptation as you approach retirement, and the skillful navigation of economic downturns while fortifying your financial citadel.

Balancing Growth and Preservation

The journey of wealth creation often starts with the quest for growth, an earnest endeavor to turn modest investments into substantial assets. However, as time bestows its wisdom, the narrative transitions. The pursuit of growth doesn't abate, but it intertwines with the preservation of what has been achieved. Balancing these two aspects is akin to conducting a symphony, where each instrument, though distinct, harmonizes to create a sublime composition.

In the realm of investment decisions, this balance is akin to maintaining a diversified portfolio. While seeking avenues of growth such as stocks and high-yield bonds, it's equally crucial to allocate a portion to more stable investments like government bonds or real estate. This blend not only mitigates risk but also ensures that your financial well-being remains resilient in the face of market fluctuations.

Adaptation as Retirement Beckons

The sunset of one's career, often accompanied by the dawn of retirement, marks a transformational juncture in the wealth journey. The strategies that served you well during the accumulation phase might require recalibration. The canvas of your financial landscape changes, as a more conservative approach gains prominence to secure the gains of years past.

As you approach retirement, the focus shifts from the aggressive pursuit of growth to the preservation of your capital. Asset allocation becomes paramount. Redistributing your investments to include more income-generating and low-risk options can provide a steady stream of funds to meet your evolving needs. Moreover, considering annuities or long-term bonds can offer a dependable source of income during your retirement years.

Safeguarding Wealth Amid Economic Tempests

Just as a seasoned sailor prepares for storms at sea, a prudent investor anticipates economic downturns. These periods of turbulence can test the mettle of even the most seasoned financiers. But fear not, for with foresight and strategic planning, you can navigate these tempests and emerge with your financial stronghold fortified.

During economic downturns, preserving wealth doesn't necessarily mean stagnation. Instead, it implies a tactical retreat rather than a full-scale retreat. While the markets may experience volatility, opportunities for astute investments often arise. It is during these times that assets may be undervalued, paving the way for shrewd investors to purchase at a discount.

Diversification, the evergreen strategy, plays a pivotal role in weathering economic storms. A well-diversified portfolio is akin to a well-structured fortress, impervious to single market shocks. Moreover, maintaining an emergency fund ensures that you have a buffer against unexpected expenses without liquidating your core investments.

As you navigate the complexities of long-term wealth preservation, remember that this journey isn't solely about you. It extends to the generations that follow—a legacy etched not just in monetary assets but in the wisdom you impart. The torch of financial stewardship passes from your hands to those of your heirs, and with it, the responsibility to safeguard and continue the legacy you've built.

The pursuit of long-term wealth preservation demands a blend of vigilance, strategy, and adaptability. Just as an artist preserves a masterpiece for generations to come, your role as a financial maestro involves safeguarding the fruits of your labor. As you approach this chapter of your financial narrative, remember that the symphony of growth and preservation is one that reverberates through time, leaving an indelible mark on your own life and those that follow.

Chapter 6: Tax Efficiency Strategies

Understanding Taxation

In the intricate dance of financial management, taxes play a central role—a role that often shapes the contours of our financial landscapes more than we might initially realize. The symphony of different types of taxes, the ever-shifting cadence of tax laws, and the pursuit of tax optimization create a complex melody that every astute investor and wealth strategist must learn to harmonize with.

Knowledge of Different Types of Taxes

To truly grasp the nuances of taxation, it is imperative to familiarize oneself with the range of taxes that influence our financial choices. Among the key players are income taxes, capital gains taxes, and estate taxes. Each tax serves as a unique note in the fiscal composition, impacting the way wealth is accumulated, preserved, and passed on.

Income Taxes: Arguably the most familiar note in the taxation symphony, income taxes are levied on an individual's earnings—wages, salaries, dividends, and other sources of income. Understanding your effective tax rate, which is the percentage of your income paid in taxes, is vital. Additionally, recognizing the distinction between ordinary income and long-term capital gains is pivotal, as capital gains are typically taxed at lower rates.

Capital Gains Taxes: The rhythm of investing echoes in the world of capital gains taxes. When you sell an asset, such as stocks, real estate, or other investments, the difference between your purchase price and selling price constitutes a capital gain. These gains can be short-term or long-term, with different tax rates applying to each. The art lies in strategic timing to minimize your tax liability.

Estate Taxes: While often discussed less frequently, estate taxes exert a profound influence on wealth transition. When assets are passed from one generation to another, they may be subject to estate taxes. The importance of estate planning, including the use of trusts and other legal tools, cannot be overstated, as they can mitigate the impact of these taxes, enabling smoother wealth transfer.

Staying Current on Tax Laws
Tax laws are akin to the tides—constantly ebbing and flowing, shaping the contours of our financial shorelines. Staying updated on these changes is more than just an intellectual exercise; it's a practical necessity. Tax codes evolve, adapting to economic shifts, political landscapes, and societal needs. The tax landscape can experience substantial shifts due to changes in administration, economic crises, and technological advancements.

Failing to stay current on tax laws can have significant consequences. You might miss out on potential deductions, credits, or other benefits that could be leveraged to optimize your financial position. Moreover, certain opportunities, such as tax-advantaged accounts, could pass you by. It's a dynamic landscape that necessitates ongoing education, whether through consultation with tax professionals, reading reputable financial publications, or attending seminars.

Seeking Professional Advice for Tax Optimization
In the symphony of tax management, seeking professional advice is akin to having a skilled conductor guiding the orchestra. Tax laws can be intricate, nuanced, and overwhelming to the untrained ear. As such, enlisting the services of tax professionals, accountants, and financial advisors can elevate your financial performance to a higher level of sophistication.

Tax professionals possess the expertise to navigate complex tax codes, identify deductions and credits, and optimize your tax strategy. They can analyze your financial profile, provide insights into areas of improvement, and keep you abreast of regulatory changes that may impact your tax planning. This partnership can help you make informed decisions while ensuring compliance with tax laws.

Understanding taxation is not merely a matter of financial literacy; it is an art form that requires continuous learning and strategic orchestration. Your ability to harmonize different types of taxes, stay attuned to evolving tax laws, and seek professional guidance will empower you to create a symphony of financial success that resounds for generations to come. As we proceed through this journey, remember that taxation is not an obstacle to wealth; it's a

dynamic landscape you can navigate with skill and
precision.

Tax Advantaged Accounts

In the realm of wealth management, few aspects hold as
much significance as understanding the nuances of
taxation. As we traverse the intricate pathways of financial
strategy, we inevitably encounter the subject of taxes—both
a necessary contribution to society and a terrain ripe for
strategic optimization. Welcome to a sub-chapter that
unveils the realm of tax-advantaged accounts—a treasure
trove of opportunities to shield your hard-earned assets
from the grasp of excessive taxation.

Exploring the Landscape of Tax-Advantaged Accounts

Within the realm of tax efficiency, tax-advantaged accounts
stand as gleaming citadels of financial prudence. These
accounts are not only conduits for safeguarding your wealth
but also avenues for fostering growth without the erosive
touch of taxation. At their core, tax-advantaged accounts
offer a mechanism to incentivize saving, investing, and
preparing for the future.

401(k)s: The Backbone of Retirement Planning

Among the most iconic pillars of tax-advantaged accounts stands the 401(k). These employer-sponsored retirement plans form the bedrock upon which many individuals build their retirement dreams. One of their most alluring aspects is the concept of deferred taxation—a practice that enables you to contribute pre-tax dollars, thus reducing your current taxable income. This deferral culminates in a double advantage: immediate tax savings and the power of compounding over time.

Within this realm, however, lies a jewel of even greater value—the employer match. Often, employers offer to match a percentage of your contributions, effectively giving you a financial boost on top of your own savings. This is a match made in financial heaven, a gesture that, if left unutilized, amounts to forfeiting free money.

IRAs: A Personal Haven for Tax Efficiency

While 401(k)s shine as workplace treasures, Individual Retirement Accounts (IRAs) offer a personal haven for those who seek tax efficiency on their own terms. Whether you opt for a Traditional IRA or a Roth IRA, both bear the gift of tax benefits, though each comes with its own flavor of advantage.

A Traditional IRA operates similarly to a 401(k) in that contributions are tax-deductible, potentially lowering your taxable income today. The catch lies in the future, where withdrawals during retirement are subject to taxation. In contrast, a Roth IRA operates in the reverse order: contributions are made with post-tax dollars, but the withdrawals during retirement are blissfully tax-free. The decision between the two hinges on your current financial situation, future projections, and your comfort level with tax strategies.

HSAs: A Unique Triple-Tax Advantage

As we explore the landscape of tax-advantaged accounts, an often underestimated champion emerges—the Health Savings Account (HSA). While not exclusive to retirement, HSAs carry a triple-tax advantage that is nothing short of remarkable.

Here's the trifecta of benefits: Contributions are tax-deductible, earnings grow tax-free, and withdrawals are tax-free when used for qualified medical expenses. An HSA thus performs the artful feat of simultaneously minimizing your tax burden and safeguarding your health-related financial well-being.

Maximizing Contributions

In the realm of tax-advantaged accounts, a cardinal rule echoes through the corridors of financial wisdom— maximize your contributions. By contributing the maximum allowed amount to your 401(k), IRA, or HSA, you amplify your ability to harness the power of tax-deferred growth. The larger the sum nestled within these accounts, the more robustly compounding interest can work its magic, steadily cultivating a pool of wealth that is both shielded from immediate taxation and poised to blossom during your retirement years.

Leveraging Tax-Deferred Growth for Retirement
At the heart of tax-advantaged accounts lies a potent force—tax-deferred growth. The power of compounding interest becomes magnified within these accounts, where your contributions can flourish and multiply without the immediate deduction of taxes. This concept is especially poignant in the context of retirement planning.

Imagine this: your contributions to a 401(k) or a Traditional IRA are akin to seeds sown in fertile soil. As time elapses, these seeds germinate into robust financial plants, with each year's growth building upon the previous. During this process, your investments generate returns that compound upon themselves—a phenomenon amplified by the absence of annual tax deductions. This tax-deferred growth can result in a more substantial retirement fund than if the same investments were held in a taxable account.

In essence, by leveraging tax-deferred growth, you are granting your future self a valuable gift—an ample financial cushion to enjoy the golden years without the burden of immediate taxation.

The art of tax efficiency demands a careful ballet—a dance between your current financial needs and your future aspirations. The key is to strike a balance, to leverage these accounts strategically, and to align your contributions with your overarching financial plan.

In the realm of finance, taxes are a reality, but their impact can be tempered through careful planning and an adept understanding of the tax-advantaged accounts at your disposal. Remember, each financial decision is a brushstroke on the canvas of your fiscal destiny—let tax efficiency be the palette that paints a masterpiece of wealth preservation and growth.

Tax-Efficient Investment Strategies

Taxes often emerge as a pivotal partner, exerting their influence on the overall composition of your financial portfolio. Tax-efficient investment strategies, often regarded as the guardian angels of your hard-earned money, play a crucial role in optimizing your financial outcomes and ensuring that every dollar you earn is directed toward your goals rather than the taxman's coffers.

Minimizing Capital Gains through Strategic Asset Allocation

Capital gains—those fruits of your investment endeavors— can be both a source of pride and a source of taxes. However, they can also be strategically managed to lessen their impact on your bottom line. One of the most powerful tools in your arsenal is strategic asset allocation.

Imagine your investment portfolio as a diverse garden, each asset class representing a unique plant. By periodically rebalancing your portfolio, you can trim the overgrown winners (which often come with higher capital gains) and nurture the underperformers. This process not only ensures that your investments align with your risk tolerance but also strategically manages your capital gains.

In essence, rather than letting gains accumulate unchecked, strategic asset allocation allows you to control the timing of realized gains. By thoughtfully rebalancing your portfolio, you can harvest losses to offset gains, thereby minimizing the tax liability arising from your investments' success.

Utilizing Tax-Efficient Funds and Strategies
Just as an artisan selects the finest tools to craft their masterpiece, astute investors harness tax-efficient funds and strategies to craft their financial success story. Enter index funds and exchange-traded funds (ETFs), the unsung heroes of tax efficiency.

These funds are designed to replicate the performance of market indices, offering diversification and the potential for steady returns. Yet, their true magic lies in their tax-efficient nature. Unlike actively managed funds that frequently buy and sell securities, incurring capital gains along the way, index funds and ETFs typically experience lower turnover. This translates to fewer capital gains distributions, which means less taxable income for you, the investor.

Additionally, consider tax-loss harvesting—a technique where you strategically sell underperforming assets to offset realized gains. This not only lowers your immediate tax bill but can also be carried forward to offset future gains. Employed with finesse, tax-loss harvesting can serve as a powerful mechanism to turn market volatility to your advantage.

Charitable Giving for Tax Benefits and Social Impact
In the realm of tax efficiency, the synergy between financial strategy and social impact emerges as an extraordinary opportunity. Charitable giving, often perceived as a virtuous act, also carries with it substantial tax benefits.

Strategically aligning your philanthropic inclinations with your financial objectives can yield both emotional and financial rewards. By donating appreciated assets such as stocks or real estate, you not only contribute to causes dear to your heart but also sidestep capital gains tax that would have been incurred had you sold the assets.

Furthermore, by establishing charitable trusts or donor-advised funds, you gain the flexibility to time your donations in a manner that optimizes your tax deductions. The funds allocated to these entities can grow tax-free while you determine the most opportune moments to make contributions.

Tax-efficient investment strategies are a testament to the artistry of finance—an artistry that seeks to protect your wealth while aligning your values and aspirations. By understanding the nuances of asset allocation, embracing tax-efficient funds, and weaving charitable giving into your financial tapestry, you elevate your journey toward financial mastery.

The path to tax efficiency is not one of evasion but of strategic navigation, where informed decisions align with your goals and values. With every dollar saved through these strategies, you empower yourself to further your financial ambitions and contribute to a world of positive change.

Chapter 7: Wealth Preservation through Estate Planning

Estate Planning Fundamentals

In the symphony of financial management, estate planning resonates as a harmonious chord that bridges the present with the future, weaving a tapestry of security and legacy. It is within the realm of estate planning that we address the inevitable truth that, while our mortal existence is finite, the impact of our actions can transcend generations. In this sub-chapter, we embark on an exploration of estate planning fundamentals—stepping stones that pave the way for the preservation of your hard-earned wealth, the protection of your loved ones, and the cultivation of a lasting legacy.

Crafting a Will: A Testament to Your Intentions

At the cornerstone of estate planning stands the venerable instrument of the last will and testament. This document, carefully drafted and legally binding, serves as a beacon of clarity, illuminating your wishes and instructions for the distribution of your assets upon your passing. A will extends beyond the realm of wealth; it speaks to your values, your relationships, and your dreams for the future.

Within the confines of a well-constructed will, the allocation of your assets assumes a strategic significance. The process of drafting a will invites introspection—a meditation on what you hold dear and how you envision your loved ones benefiting from your life's work. Through the concise language of your will, you designate beneficiaries, ensuring that your wealth reaches the hands you deem deserving.

While the process of crafting a will may sound straightforward, its significance is immeasurable. Many have discovered the hard way that failing to document their intentions can lead to protracted legal battles and emotional turmoil for their loved ones. Thus, as you engage in the act of estate planning, remember that a meticulously drafted will is not only a gift to yourself but a gesture of consideration towards those you cherish.

Trusts: Sculpting Your Legacy with Precision
Beyond the boundaries of a will, trusts emerge as instruments of intricate design, imbued with the power to tailor the distribution of assets to your exact specifications. Trusts offer a level of control that extends even beyond the veil of mortality. They provide an avenue to nurture philanthropic endeavors, support beneficiaries with special needs, and cultivate the financial growth of younger generations.

The act of establishing a trust involves the appointment of a trustee—a fiduciary entrusted with the solemn responsibility of managing the assets in accordance with the trust's terms. While there are various types of trusts, each possessing distinct benefits and purposes, they all share a common thread: the ability to navigate complex financial landscapes with finesse.

Guardianship: Nurturing the Well-being of Dependents
Within the framework of estate planning lies a facet that
extends beyond the realm of financial assets—the
guardianship of your dependents. For those with minor
children, the question of who would care for them in the
event of your untimely passing is a profound one. Through
the designation of legal guardians in your estate planning
documents, you ensure that your children are entrusted to
individuals who share your values and aspirations for their
future.

Choosing guardians requires a thoughtful evaluation of not
only your potential nominees' ability to provide care but
also their compatibility with your familial ethos. Consider
their moral compass, financial stability, and capacity to
provide emotional support to your children during what
would undoubtedly be a challenging time.

As we draw the curtain on this exploration of estate
planning fundamentals, we recognize that this sub-chapter
represents not only a pragmatic undertaking but a testament
to your commitment to the well-being of your loved ones.
By crafting a will, establishing trusts, and designating
guardians, you craft a legacy of intentions—a roadmap that
ensures your wishes are fulfilled and your impact
reverberates through the lives of those you hold dear.

Estate planning, though it delves into the contemplation of
mortality, is an affirmation of life. It transcends the realm
of material wealth, resonating with the vibrancy of the
relationships you cherish and the values you wish to

perpetuate. Remember that estate planning is a dynamic process, one that evolves as your circumstances change and your aspirations grow.

As we journey forward through the intricacies of wealth preservation, let the act of estate planning serve as a poignant reminder of your capacity to shape the future—a future enriched by your foresight, your care, and your commitment to the well-being of generations to come.

Minimizing Estate Taxes

In the intricate landscape of wealth preservation, few challenges loom larger than the specter of estate taxes. As we navigate the realm of estate planning, this sub-chapter illuminates a crucial facet: the art of minimizing estate taxes. While taxation is an inevitable reality, strategic planning can significantly mitigate its impact, ensuring that your hard-earned assets are preserved for the benefit of your loved ones and philanthropic endeavors.

Understanding Estate Tax Thresholds and Exemptions

Estate taxes, often referred to as the "death tax," are levied on the transfer of wealth from one generation to the next. The first step in minimizing these taxes is to comprehend the intricate web of thresholds and exemptions that dictate their application.

Estate tax laws vary across jurisdictions, and it's vital to be well-versed in the rules specific to your location. Many jurisdictions establish a threshold beyond which estates become subject to taxation. This threshold is often referred to as the "exemption limit." Estates below this limit are exempt from estate taxes, while those exceeding it are subjected to varying tax rates.

Keep in mind that tax laws evolve, and staying informed about potential changes is imperative. Engage legal and financial experts who specialize in estate planning to help you navigate this dynamic landscape.

Utilizing Gifting Strategies to Reduce Taxable Estate
Gift-giving is a time-honored practice, and when leveraged strategically, it can play a pivotal role in reducing the taxable value of your estate. By gifting assets during your lifetime, you can gradually transfer wealth to your beneficiaries while simultaneously diminishing the size of your taxable estate.

One of the most powerful tools in gifting is the annual gift tax exclusion. This provision allows you to gift a certain amount of money or assets to an individual each year without incurring any gift tax liability. By doing so, you can gradually distribute your wealth to your heirs, potentially lowering the overall value of your taxable estate.

For those with a greater appetite for gifting, a lifetime gift tax exemption exists. This exemption permits individuals to gift a certain amount over their lifetime without triggering gift taxes. While it's a powerful strategy, it's crucial to be aware of the associated regulations and potential implications. Engage with legal and financial professionals to ensure your gifting strategy aligns with your overall estate plan.

Exploring Charitable Giving to Lower Estate Tax Liability
In the quest to minimize estate taxes, philanthropy emerges as an artful solution that benefits not only your legacy but also the causes you hold dear. Charitable giving allows you to channel a portion of your wealth toward worthy causes, simultaneously reducing the taxable value of your estate.

One effective method is the establishment of a charitable remainder trust. This trust permits you to transfer assets into a trust, with beneficiaries receiving income from the trust for a specified period. After this period, the remaining assets are donated to a charitable organization of your choice. This strategy provides both an income stream and tax benefits while supporting philanthropic causes.

Another approach is the creation of a charitable lead trust. In this arrangement, the charitable organization receives income from the trust for a predetermined period. Once this period concludes, the remaining assets are transferred to your beneficiaries. This strategy can yield estate tax deductions while benefiting both philanthropy and heirs.

The endeavor to minimize estate taxes is not solely a pursuit of fiscal reduction; it is a testament to your commitment to creating a lasting legacy. By understanding the intricacies of estate tax thresholds, harnessing the power of gifting strategies, and embracing the potential of charitable giving, you sculpt a financial landscape that resonates with purpose and wisdom.

As you navigate the labyrinth of estate planning, remember that each decision is a brushstroke on the canvas of your legacy. Engaging with professionals who specialize in estate taxation and philanthropy can be instrumental in navigating this complex terrain. By crafting a strategy that aligns with your values and aspirations, you transform the challenge of estate taxes into an opportunity to safeguard your wealth while making a meaningful impact on the world.

Legacy Planning and Philanthropy

In the grand tapestry of life, the desire to leave a lasting imprint transcends the accumulation of wealth. It is a desire to shape the world, to sow seeds of positivity, and to contribute to the betterment of humanity. As we navigate the intricate landscape of wealth preservation through estate planning, we encounter a chapter that transcends traditional financial measures—a chapter that speaks to the very essence of who we are and what we stand for. Welcome to the realm of legacy planning and philanthropy.

Defining Your Legacy Beyond Financial Wealth

Legacy is often misconstrued as a mere transfer of material riches to the next generation. However, it encompasses a deeper, more profound concept that extends beyond the tangible. Your legacy encapsulates your values, your principles, and the mark you leave on the hearts and minds of those who follow in your footsteps.

Consider what you wish to be remembered for—what ideals you want to perpetuate long after you're gone. Is it your commitment to education, the arts, social justice, or environmental sustainability? Unearthing these core values provides the foundation for a legacy that goes beyond the finite boundaries of wealth.

Setting Up Philanthropic Endeavors and Charitable Foundations

Philanthropy is the art of leveraging resources to create positive change. It is the embodiment of our innate desire to uplift others and shape a better world. Establishing philanthropic endeavors or charitable foundations offers a structured framework to amplify your impact.

A charitable foundation, for instance, is an enduring vessel for your values. It allows you to allocate funds to causes that align with your beliefs, ensuring your philanthropic efforts continue even after you've passed. Through careful planning and governance, your charitable foundation becomes a beacon of hope, channeling resources toward initiatives that matter most to you.

Ensuring Your Values and Goals Endure Through Giving
The act of giving is not confined to financial contributions
alone. It encompasses your time, expertise, and advocacy.
By intertwining your passions with your philanthropic
endeavors, you weave a narrative that resonates with
authenticity. Engaging actively in the causes you support
allows you to witness the transformative impact firsthand,
fostering a sense of connection and purpose.

Legacy and philanthropy also extend to educating and
inspiring future generations. By involving your heirs in
charitable activities, you instill values of empathy,
responsibility, and community engagement. Your legacy
becomes a living lesson that perpetuates through your
descendants—a testament to the enduring power of
purpose-driven giving.

Navigating the Practicalities of Legacy and Philanthropy
Creating a legacy and embracing philanthropy demands
more than intention; it requires strategic planning. As you
embark on this journey, consider these practical steps:

1. Identify Your Values: Reflect on what matters most to
you. Is it education, healthcare, poverty alleviation, or
environmental sustainability? Align your philanthropy with
your passions.

2. Craft a Philanthropic Strategy: Define the scope of
your giving. Will you support local initiatives, international
causes, or a combination? Determine whether you'll focus
on a specific issue or maintain a broad approach.

3. Choose the Right Vehicle: Depending on your goals, establish a charitable foundation, donor-advised fund, or endowment. Each offers distinct advantages in terms of governance, tax benefits, and control over your giving.

4. Engage in Due Diligence: Research organizations thoroughly before directing funds. Assess their financial health, transparency, and track record in achieving impact.

5. Involve Family and Heirs: Engage your family in discussions about your philanthropic vision. Encourage their input and ensure alignment with your values.

6. Seek Professional Guidance: Consult legal and financial advisors experienced in philanthropic planning. They can help structure your giving to maximize impact and tax benefits.

A Legacy Beyond Measure
As you embark on the path of legacy planning and philanthropy, remember that your influence transcends monetary value. Your legacy is a tapestry woven from the threads of empathy, compassion, and purpose. Through your giving, you extend a lifeline to those in need, leaving an indelible mark on the world.

The convergence of wealth preservation and philanthropy is a testament to the multifaceted nature of true prosperity. By crafting a legacy that reflects your values, you navigate the waves of time and leave ripples that echo through generations. Embrace this chapter as an opportunity to redefine success, and let your legacy shine as a beacon of inspiration for those who follow.

Chapter 8: Navigating Economic Challenges

Recession-Proofing Your Finances

In the vast tapestry of economic cycles, recessions stand as unavoidable threads that weave through the fabric of financial markets. Like the ebb and flow of tides, economic downturns are intrinsic to the growth trajectory of any economy. Yet, despite their inevitability, the looming specter of recession often instills a sense of uncertainty and unease in individuals and businesses alike.

In this sub-chapter, we delve into the art of "recession-proofing" your finances—a skill set that goes beyond merely surviving economic turbulence. It involves a strategic blend of preparedness, adaptability, and prudent decision-making to not only weather the storm but also seize opportunities amid the tempest.

Building an Emergency Fund for Financial Stability

The cornerstone of recession-proofing is the establishment of an emergency fund—a financial fortress that shields you from unforeseen adversities. This fund serves as a bulwark against sudden job loss, medical emergencies, or unexpected expenses, allowing you to navigate challenging times without resorting to debt or liquidating long-term investments.

A rule of thumb suggests that your emergency fund should ideally cover three to six months' worth of living expenses. This cushion provides a safety net during uncertain periods, enabling you to focus on strategic decisions rather than

scrambling for immediate financial solutions. Whether
you're an individual or a business, prioritizing the creation
and maintenance of an emergency fund lays a solid
foundation for navigating economic challenges.

**Identifying Recession-Resistant Industries and
Investments**

While it's impossible to entirely shield oneself from the
impact of a recession, certain industries and investments
tend to display a degree of resilience. Consider sectors like
healthcare, utilities, and essential consumer goods—these
areas of the economy often demonstrate relatively stable
demand even during economic downturns.

When constructing your investment portfolio, diversifying
across recession-resistant sectors can mitigate risk. Real
estate, particularly rental properties, can offer a steady
stream of income even in turbulent times. Bonds, especially
those issued by stable governments or corporations, can
provide a degree of security. However, remember that no
investment is entirely immune to economic shifts; the key
lies in a balanced and well-informed approach.

**Strategies for Staying Afloat During Economic
Downturns**

As the tempest of recession rages, strategic navigation
becomes paramount. Businesses must pivot their strategies
to adapt to changing consumer behavior, while individuals
need to adopt prudent financial habits to weather the storm.

During these periods, preserving capital takes precedence over aggressive expansion.

For businesses, this might involve revisiting expenditure priorities, renegotiating contracts, and exploring cost-saving measures. Adapting to new market realities and identifying underserved niches can also open avenues for growth. Similarly, individuals should prioritize essentials and delay discretionary spending, while also exploring supplementary income streams through freelancing or part-time work.

The economic landscape during a recession is akin to a turbulent sea, yet amid the waves lie hidden opportunities. Stocks of strong companies may become undervalued, offering potential for future growth when markets rebound. The real estate market may present opportunities for property acquisition at lower prices. However, seizing these opportunities requires astute market analysis and a long-term perspective.

Recession-proofing is not about evading economic downturns but about fortifying your financial foundation to withstand their impact. It's a testament to your preparedness and adaptability in the face of uncertainty. The key is to build a robust emergency fund, diversify your investments, and cultivate strategic resilience in both personal and business finances. Just as a well-constructed ship navigates through storms, your financial acumen will guide you through the economic ebbs and flows with confidence and foresight.

Thriving During Market Volatility

In the vast landscape of financial markets, volatility is both an inevitable force and an enigmatic phenomenon. It has the power to stir emotions ranging from apprehension to exhilaration, often in the span of a single trading day. As we delve into the art of thriving during market volatility, we embark on a crucial journey—one that encompasses not only the practical strategies of navigating turbulent waters but also the psychological fortitude required to emerge unscathed and even enriched.

Maintaining a Long-Term Perspective in Volatile Markets

Picture a ship navigating the tumultuous seas. Amidst crashing waves and unpredictable currents, the captain remains resolute, steering with a steady hand towards the distant shore. In much the same way, maintaining a long-term perspective in volatile markets is akin to possessing the captain's unwavering determination. Market fluctuations, whether caused by geopolitical events, economic data releases, or investor sentiment, can cause short-term panic and euphoria. Yet, beneath the tempestuous surface lies the enduring truth that markets tend to regain equilibrium over time.

In the face of rapid price swings, the seasoned investor keeps their eyes fixed on their long-term goals. It's important to recognize that while market volatility can erode short-term gains, it seldom alters the fundamental value of well-established investments. By embracing a patient approach, you shield yourself from the impulse to make rash decisions driven by short-term emotions. This perspective allows you to ride out the storms with an unshakable belief in the resilience of the markets.

Diversification as a Shield Against Market Turbulence
Imagine an archer with an assortment of arrows, each designed for a specific purpose. Similarly, a well-constructed investment portfolio is akin to an array of arrows, each representing a different asset class or sector. Diversification is the art of spreading your investments across a spectrum of assets, which acts as a shield against the concentrated risks that can emerge during market volatility.

When one sector falters, another might thrive, offering a buffer against losses. Diversification also extends to geographical regions and investment types. By holding a mix of stocks, bonds, real estate, and possibly alternative investments, you ensure that your portfolio isn't overly exposed to the movements of a single market.

In times of volatility, the diversified investor finds solace in the fact that the performance of their entire portfolio isn't hinging on the fate of a single asset. This strategic allocation, while not eliminating risk, certainly mitigates its impact, providing a sense of stability even when the market landscape appears tumultuous.

Seizing Investment Opportunities During Market Dips

Contrary to conventional wisdom, market volatility can be a wellspring of opportunity for the discerning investor. Picture a clearance sale, where high-quality merchandise is temporarily available at discounted prices. In the world of investing, market dips often present a similar opportunity to acquire valuable assets at lower-than-usual prices. This practice, known as "buying the dip," requires both courage and strategic acumen.

When the market experiences a downturn, it's natural for fear to cloud rational judgment. However, those who have mastered the art of seizing investment opportunities understand that these downturns are part of the market's natural ebb and flow. Such investors keep a watchful eye on their target assets, awaiting moments when market sentiment overshadows intrinsic value. By doing so, they position themselves to accumulate assets at favorable prices, setting the stage for potential gains when markets eventually recover.

In the grand theater of finance, market volatility plays the role of both antagonist and ally. It challenges our composure, tests our resolve, and invites us to demonstrate our commitment to long-term financial objectives. Through maintaining a long-term perspective, embracing diversification, and seizing opportunities during market dips, investors can not only navigate the stormy seas of volatility but also transform these tempestuous moments into stepping stones toward financial prosperity. Remember, in times of volatility, it is the well-prepared and

the resolute who stand the best chance of not merely
surviving, but thriving.

Adapting to Technological Disruption

In the grand tapestry of human progress, few forces have
woven as intricate a pattern of transformation as
technology. As we delve into the heart of navigating
economic challenges, we find ourselves standing at the
crossroads of an era characterized by rapid technological
advancement. In this sub chapter, we venture into the realm
of adapting to technological disruption—a realm where
innovation begetss opportunities, and adaptability becomes
the currency of success.

Embracing Technological Advancements for Financial Growth

In an age where innovation unfolds at a breathtaking pace,
the prudent wealth strategist recognizes that technology is
more than just a tool; it's a catalyst for exponential growth.
Embracing technology in your financial journey is not
merely a choice; it is an imperative. Technological tools
and platforms can empower you to streamline investment
processes, monitor financial health in real-time, and make
data-driven decisions.

Financial technology, or "fintech," has democratized access
to investment opportunities, making it possible for
individuals to engage in activities previously reserved for

financial professionals. Automated investment platforms, also known as robo-advisors, provide tailored investment recommendations based on algorithms, minimizing human bias and optimizing portfolio performance. Additionally, digital payment systems, blockchain technology, and cryptocurrencies have disrupted traditional financial systems, presenting alternative avenues for wealth accumulation and preservation.

Identifying Industries Poised for Technological Disruption

Amidst the waves of innovation, certain industries emerge as harbors for technological disruption. As a financial steward, the onus is on you to discern these opportunities and leverage them to your advantage. Industries such as artificial intelligence, renewable energy, biotechnology, and e-commerce have not only transformed economies but also altered the dynamics of wealth creation.

Artificial intelligence, for instance, has revolutionized data analysis, predictive modeling, and customer service, leading to enhanced investment strategies and risk assessment. The rise of renewable energy technologies presents not only environmentally conscious investment opportunities but also the potential for long-term financial gains as the world shifts toward sustainable practices. Staying attuned to these trends and assessing their alignment with your financial goals can position you at the forefront of wealth creation.

Upgrading Skills to Stay Relevant in Changing Job Markets

As technology reshapes industries, it simultaneously reshapes the skillsets demanded by the job market. The ability to adapt and learn new skills is a linchpin in remaining relevant in a landscape defined by change. As a proactive investor in your own potential, consider upskilling and reskilling to match the demands of emerging industries.

Online education platforms, workshops, and certifications offer flexible avenues for acquiring new proficiencies. Learning coding languages, data analysis techniques, or digital marketing strategies can equip you with skills applicable across industries. By investing in your skill portfolio, you not only enhance your employability but also position yourself to leverage the opportunities arising from technological disruption.

As we traverse the territory of technological disruption, remember that every wave of innovation carries the promise of both challenge and growth. Embracing technology not only enhances your financial acumen but also broadens your horizons. By recognizing industries primed for transformation and adapting your skills accordingly, you place yourself in a position of advantage—one that allows you to ride the crest of technological progress rather than be overwhelmed by its force.

The path to financial mastery weaves through the digital realm, where data-driven decisions and adaptability become your compass. As technology continues to shape our world, let it be a beacon guiding your choices, an enabler of your aspirations, and a key player in your journey toward financial success. In the ever-changing landscape of innovation, remember that your ability to navigate disruption becomes a testament to your resilience, resourcefulness, and ultimately, your triumph.

Chapter 9: Lifestyle Inflation and Financial Discipline

The Danger of Lifestyle Inflation

In the world of finance, where aspirations meet fiscal realities, there exists a subtle yet formidable adversary known as lifestyle inflation. It is a phenomenon that often creeps into our lives unnoticed, with consequences that can significantly impact our long-term financial well-being. In this sub-chapter, we uncover the intricate web of lifestyle inflation, exploring its pitfalls, consequences, and offering strategies to navigate this perilous terrain.

Recognizing the Pitfalls of Increasing Spending with Income

Picture this: you've worked hard, climbed the career ladder, and now find yourself with a more substantial income. Naturally, the urge to reward yourself for your accomplishments is compelling. However, the path of least resistance often leads to lifestyle inflation—a gradual increase in spending as income rises.

The trap lies in the deceptive nature of lifestyle inflation. Initially, the upgrades seem minor—a slightly fancier car, a more spacious home, a few more luxurious dining experiences. But over time, these incremental changes accumulate, casting a shadow over the financial future. The once-unconscious upgrades become expectations, and the cycle repeats itself with each income boost.

Balancing Enjoying Your Wealth with Responsible Financial Habits

The pursuit of financial success is not devoid of enjoyment. It is essential to savor the fruits of your labor and indulge in life's pleasures. However, this enjoyment must be rooted in the soil of financial responsibility.

To achieve this balance, it's crucial to distinguish between necessary and discretionary expenses. Necessary expenses encompass the essentials—shelter, food, healthcare, education—while discretionary expenses pertain to non-essential indulgences. Recognizing the boundary between these categories is the linchpin of maintaining financial equilibrium.

Strategies to Curb Unnecessary Lifestyle Inflation

1. Mindful Spending: Engage in conscious consumption. Before making a purchase, ask yourself whether it aligns with your values and long-term goals. By considering the impact of your spending, you can make choices that contribute to your financial well-being.

2. Automated Savings: Implementing automated savings mechanisms ensures that a portion of your income is allocated towards your financial goals before you even have the chance to spend it. This approach effectively prevents the entirety of income increases from being absorbed by lifestyle inflation.

3. Budgeting and Tracking: Crafting a well-defined budget serves as a compass for your financial journey.

Allocate funds for essentials, savings, and discretionary spending. Regularly track your expenses to identify potential leaks and opportunities for improvement.

4. Delayed Gratification: Practice the art of patience. Before succumbing to an impulse purchase, give yourself a cooling-off period. This delay allows time for rational thinking to prevail over momentary desires.

5. Investing in Experiences: Redirect some of your discretionary spending towards experiences that enrich your life and create lasting memories. These experiences often hold more value than material possessions and can be enjoyed without inflating your lifestyle.

6. Periodic Financial Assessments: Regularly evaluate your financial situation and progress towards your goals. This introspection helps you remain accountable and motivated, steering you away from the clutches of lifestyle inflation.

Lifestyle inflation is not a specter to be feared but rather a challenge to be confronted. By recognizing its allure and understanding its implications, you hold the power to shape your financial destiny deliberately. The road to financial independence is paved with prudent choices that encompass both indulgence and discipline.

Embrace the pleasures life has to offer, but do so with an unwavering commitment to your long-term financial well-being. With each decision, you mold not only your present but also the contours of your future. By mastering the art of taming lifestyle inflation, you transcend the cycle of consumerism and embark upon a path of lasting financial wellness—one that secures your prosperity and empowers you to achieve your dreams.

Setting Financial Boundaries

In the labyrinth of modern consumerism, where desires are marketed as needs and luxuries masquerade as necessities, setting financial boundaries is both an act of courage and a cornerstone of lasting financial success. Within the realms of this sub-chapter, we delve into the art of defining your financial priorities and goals, mastering the art of saying no to extravagant expenses, and navigating the delicate terrain of communicating your financial limits to loved ones.

Defining Your Financial Priorities and Goals

In a world teeming with options and temptations, it's remarkably easy to lose sight of what truly matters when it comes to your finances. The very first brushstroke in the canvas of financial discipline involves defining your financial priorities and goals. This isn't merely about setting arbitrary numbers or vague aspirations; it's a process of introspection that enables you to align your spending habits with your values and aspirations.

Take a moment to ponder what truly brings you joy, security, and a sense of fulfillment. Is it the prospect of owning a lavish car, or would you rather channel those resources toward traveling the world and expanding your horizons? Perhaps your heart swells with the desire to provide a solid educational foundation for your children. Whatever your aspirations, clarity is your ally.

Identify your short-term and long-term financial goals. These could range from building an emergency fund and paying off debt to purchasing a home or embarking on an entrepreneurial venture. By establishing these milestones, you not only chart your course but also inject a profound sense of purpose into your financial decisions.

Learning to Say No to Extravagant Expenses
In an era where the allure of material possessions beckons from every corner, saying no to extravagant expenses demands a steadfast commitment to your financial well-being. The truth is, every dollar spent on something superfluous is a dollar that could be invested in your future or directed toward a cause that resonates with your values.

Here's where the art of discernment comes into play. Before making a purchase, ask yourself: "Is this aligned with my goals? Does it contribute meaningfully to my life? Can I find an alternative that offers value without sacrificing quality?" By cultivating this habit of mindful spending, you protect your financial resources from dissipating into the abyss of impulsive purchases.

Communicating with Family and Friends About Your Financial Limits

Navigating the delicate waters of financial boundaries in your personal relationships can be a challenge, but it's an imperative one. Open and honest communication about your financial limits is key to ensuring that your financial decisions remain aligned with your goals. This transparency also encourages a culture of respect and understanding within your relationships.

Begin by initiating candid conversations with your loved ones. Whether it's your partner, family members, or close friends, explain your financial priorities and goals. This isn't about erecting walls or fostering a sense of aloofness; it's about sharing your perspective so that others can empathize and support your journey. When those around you understand the "why" behind your financial decisions, it's easier for them to respect your boundaries.

At times, setting boundaries might involve gracefully declining invitations to expensive events or offering alternative suggestions that align better with your goals. Remember, the goal isn't to alienate, but to foster an environment where your financial discipline is respected and where shared experiences hold more value than opulent displays.

The mastery of setting financial boundaries is an ongoing process that stems from a deep understanding of your values, aspirations, and the role money plays in your life. By defining your financial priorities and goals, mastering the art of saying no to excessive expenditures, and communicating your limits to loved ones, you not only fortify your financial foundation but also shape a life where purpose, intention, and financial discipline converge. The journey isn't always easy, but its rewards are immeasurable – a life sculpted by your choices, a testament to your resilience, and a legacy that extends far beyond the realm of money.

Cultivating Financial Discipline

In the intricate symphony of wealth management, one melody rises above the rest – the art of financial discipline. Picture it as the conductor orchestrating your financial endeavors, guiding every note, every expenditure, and every investment towards the crescendo of prosperity. This sub-chapter is dedicated to unraveling the nuances of cultivating financial discipline – a skill that separates those who merely tread the path of prosperity from those who waltz gracefully towards enduring financial security.

Implementing a Savings-First Mentality

In the age of instant gratification and endless temptations, the concept of delaying gratification seems almost revolutionary. Yet, it is precisely this principle that forms the cornerstone of a savings-first mentality. Rather than channeling your earnings solely into immediate desires, allocate a portion towards your financial future.

Imagine your income as a river, flowing ceaselessly. A savings-first mentality diverts a stream into reservoirs of investments and savings before allowing it to meander into day-to-day expenses. This practice establishes a crucial equilibrium between enjoying the present and securing the future. With every dollar conscientiously set aside, you're crafting a safety net for unforeseen circumstances, inching closer to your long-term aspirations, and sowing the seeds of financial resilience.

Automating Savings and Investments

Human nature is a realm of impulses and intentions, often intertwined in a delicate dance. In the realm of finance, this dance can decide the fate of your financial goals. Enter the transformative power of automation. By establishing automatic transfers from your income to savings accounts and investments, you're not just sparing yourself the deliberation of setting funds aside, but you're also ensuring consistent progress towards your financial objectives.

Consider this process as a digital assistant of sorts, diligently adhering to your predetermined plan without falter. This simple yet effective strategy not only safeguards your finances from the allure of spontaneous purchases but also instills a sense of commitment to your financial journey. The automated contributions become a non-negotiable part of your financial rhythm, gradually amplifying the symphony of your wealth accumulation.

Overcoming Impulsive Spending through Mindful Practices

In a world where consumerism reigns supreme, overcoming the allure of impulsive spending is a challenge that demands mindfulness and self-awareness. Mindfulness, in this context, entails an acute awareness of your financial goals and a conscious consideration of each expenditure's alignment with those objectives.

One practical technique is the "24-hour rule." When faced with a non-essential purchase, give yourself the gift of time – a full day to reflect before committing. This pause grants you the clarity to differentiate between a genuine need and an impulsive desire. Additionally, create a personal spending mantra. This succinct phrase acts as a guardian of your financial aspirations, reminding you of the bigger picture when the allure of instant gratification beckons.

Beyond these techniques, self-reflection is your greatest ally. Understand the emotional triggers behind impulsive spending. Are you seeking comfort, validation, or fleeting joy? Identifying these triggers empowers you to address the root cause rather than succumbing to momentary indulgence.

In the realm of personal finance, discipline is not synonymous with deprivation. Instead, it's a harmonious balance between short-term pleasures and long-term security. Cultivating financial discipline enriches your life with the freedom to make choices aligned with your goals, rather than merely reacting to circumstances.

As you embark on this journey, remember that financial discipline is a skill that evolves with practice. The path may not always be linear; there might be occasional stumbles. Yet, those who commit to its cultivation find themselves crafting a life adorned with not just material abundance, but also the tranquility that stems from knowing their financial house is built on solid ground.

Harness the power of a savings-first mentality, embrace the automation that propels your progress, and infuse every purchase with mindfulness. As you do, you're not just orchestrating a symphony of discipline, but composing the masterpiece of your financial success. This is the essence of the art of financial discipline – a masterpiece that resonates through time, building bridges between your aspirations and reality.

Chapter 10: Maximizing Income Potential

Negotiating Your Worth

In the modern age of financial empowerment, few skills are as pivotal as the art of negotiation. It's a skill that encapsulates the essence of maximizing your income potential, and one that transcends industries, professions, and backgrounds. Whether you find yourself in a corporate boardroom or at the helm of your entrepreneurial venture, the ability to negotiate effectively can spell the difference between modest compensation and an impactful, rewarding financial journey.

Strategies for Negotiating Salary and Benefits

Negotiation, at its core, is a dance between aspiration and collaboration. It's a delicate balance of asserting your value while fostering a mutually beneficial agreement. Imagine a chessboard where each move is a calculated step towards your financial goals. When it comes to your salary and benefits, this is not the time for modesty; it's the time to present a compelling case for your worth.

Strategically negotiating your salary and benefits can set the trajectory for your entire financial journey. The first step is understanding that negotiation is not merely an event; it's a process. Approach it with meticulous preparation and a deep understanding of your unique value proposition.

Showcasing Your Value

Before entering the negotiation arena, take a moment to reflect on your accomplishments, skills, and the unique perspective you bring to the table. Remember, it's not just about the job you're performing; it's about the impact you're making. Have you increased efficiency, boosted revenue, or brought innovation to your role? Compile a portfolio of your achievements and contributions. This portfolio will serve as the foundation upon which you'll build your case.

While numbers are a universal language, don't underestimate the power of storytelling. Narratives that highlight how you've tackled challenges, led teams, and transformed processes can leave a lasting impression. Your goal is to not only demonstrate what you've achieved but also to illustrate how you've made a difference. This is how you transition from being an employee to becoming an invaluable asset.

The Role of Education: Elevating Your Earning Potential

In the realm of financial growth, education is the catalyst that propels you forward. Continuous learning isn't a mere luxury; it's a necessity. As industries evolve and paradigms shift, acquiring new skills and knowledge becomes a strategic advantage. It's no surprise that those who invest in their education often find themselves positioned for higher income opportunities.

Enrolling in courses, attending workshops, and pursuing certifications relevant to your field showcase your commitment to growth. They signify your adaptability, a trait highly valued in today's dynamic professional landscape. By staying attuned to emerging trends and expanding your skill set, you demonstrate your dedication to both personal development and contributing to your organization's success.

Walking the Path: Key Considerations

As you embark on the journey of negotiation, consider these key considerations:

- **Research and Benchmarking**: Understand the industry standards for your role and location. Research what others in similar positions are earning. This knowledge serves as a foundation for your negotiation.

- **Timing and Context**: Timing is crucial. Negotiate after you've demonstrated your value and contributions, such as after successful projects or performance reviews. Additionally, consider the context of the company's financial health and current economic climate.

- **Listening and Flexibility**: Negotiation is a dialogue, not a monologue. Listen to the needs and concerns of the other party. Be open to compromise while keeping your key priorities in mind.

- **Confidence and Professionalism**: Confidence in your abilities is magnetic. Present yourself with poise and professionalism. Maintain eye contact, speak clearly, and convey your points with conviction.

The journey of negotiating your worth is one of empowerment and self-advocacy. It's not about demanding; it's about demonstrating the value you bring to the table. By weaving together the threads of your achievements, skills, and ongoing education, you construct a compelling narrative that showcases your worth.

Negotiation is a skill that extends beyond the realm of your professional life. It's a tool that can impact various aspects of your financial journey, from securing a better starting salary to improving the terms of an investment deal. As you delve into the art of negotiation, recognize that it's a skill that evolves with practice. Each negotiation is an opportunity to refine your approach, learn from the process, and emerge as a more effective advocate for your financial aspirations.

Side Hustles and Freelancing

In an era where the traditional career landscape is evolving at an unprecedented pace, the notion of relying solely on a single job for financial security has begun to shift. The concept of side hustles and freelancing has emerged as a dynamic force, offering individuals the opportunity to leverage their unique skills, passions, and talents to generate additional streams of income. Welcome to a realm where your hobbies, expertise, and innovative thinking can pave the way to a more secure and prosperous financial future.

The Art of Identifying Marketable Skills

One of the most significant advantages of embracing side hustles and freelancing is the freedom to harness your distinct abilities and turn them into revenue-generating endeavors. As you venture into this realm, the first step is to identify your marketable skills. These skills are the currency that will propel your side hustle or freelance venture forward. Take time to introspect and assess your strengths, talents, and areas of expertise.

In the modern landscape, marketable skills encompass a diverse range. From content creation, graphic design, and web development to social media management, copywriting, and online tutoring, the possibilities are vast. The key lies in understanding not just your proficiency in a particular skill but also its demand in the market. Consider conducting research to pinpoint industries or niches where your expertise can truly shine.

Launching and Nurturing Successful Side Businesses

Turning a marketable skill into a thriving side business demands a combination of strategic planning, dedication, and adaptability. Once you've identified your skill, begin by crafting a clear vision for your venture. Define your target audience, the unique value you offer, and the problems your service or product solves. This foundation will serve as the cornerstone of your marketing efforts and customer engagement.

The digital landscape has bestowed upon us an array of platforms to showcase our talents and products. From launching an e-commerce store to offering services on freelance platforms or even creating an online course, your options are virtually limitless. It's imperative to cultivate a strong online presence through engaging websites, social media platforms, and content that not only highlights your skill but also resonates with your potential clients.

Managing Multiple Income Streams
As you navigate the realm of side hustles and freelancing, it's crucial to strike a delicate balance between your primary occupation and your supplementary income-generating activities. While the allure of additional income is enticing, overextending yourself could lead to burnout and diminished performance across all fronts. Therefore, meticulous time management becomes paramount.

Create a well-defined schedule that allocates specific time blocks for your side hustle or freelance work. This practice not only enhances your efficiency but also ensures that your main job doesn't suffer. Moreover, consider the financial aspect of your endeavors. While extra income is indeed a boon, it's wise to allocate a portion toward savings, taxes, and personal investments.

The Ripple Effect: Financial Security and Growth

As your side hustle or freelance venture gains momentum, a remarkable transformation begins to unfold—one that extends beyond mere financial gain. Diversifying your income sources infuses your financial profile with resilience. Multiple streams of income provide a cushion against economic uncertainties, offering a safeguard during challenging times.

Additionally, the pursuit of side hustles often fosters a sense of autonomy, creativity, and continuous learning. It encourages you to evolve, adapt, and explore new opportunities. The knowledge and experience gained from your supplementary endeavors can even propel your main career forward, as the skills you cultivate in one arena often translate into improved performance in another.

Side hustles and freelancing exemplify the fusion of innovation and entrepreneurship in the modern age. They empower individuals to harness their unique talents, transform passions into profits, and cultivate financial security through diversification. As you embark on this journey, remember that patience, dedication, and adaptability are your most steadfast companions.

Every skill you possess, every idea you nurture, and every effort you invest has the potential to catalyze a transformational shift in your financial landscape. Your side hustle isn't just an additional income stream; it's a testament to your resourcefulness and a gateway to a life

enriched by purpose, financial empowerment, and endless
possibilities.

Networking and Personal Branding

In the intricate tapestry of wealth creation and career
advancement, networking and personal branding are
threads of paramount importance. Imagine them as the
dynamic duo that wields the power to transform your
professional trajectory. While they may appear disparate,
their symbiotic relationship weaves a narrative that can
amplify your income potential and unlock a world of
opportunities.

Building a Strong Professional Network

Picture a room filled with people, each a potential
connection, collaborator, or mentor. Your network extends
beyond digital platforms and into the realm of real-life
interactions. Building a robust professional network is not a
mere collection of business cards; it's a conscious
cultivation of relationships that enrich your professional
life.

A diverse network introduces you to fresh perspectives,
novel ideas, and uncharted avenues. It connects you to
professionals from various industries, backgrounds, and
experiences. Like a web spun across industries, your
network can bridge gaps, facilitate introductions, and
unearth prospects that would otherwise remain concealed.

Begin with authenticity. Authentic connections are enduring connections. Seek opportunities to engage with peers and mentors in settings conducive to meaningful conversations. Attend industry events, seminars, workshops, and conferences. Engage in dialogues that demonstrate your genuine curiosity and passion for your field.

Remember, quality triumphs over quantity. Fostering deep connections with a handful of individuals who align with your goals can be more beneficial than amassing a large but superficial network. Strive to leave a lasting impression, one that resonates not just with your expertise, but with your character and values as well.

Leveraging Social Media for Personal Branding
In the digital age, your online presence is often the first glimpse into your professional persona. Enter the realm of personal branding—a venture that's not about becoming a manufactured version of yourself, but about authentically amplifying your strengths and values.

Social media platforms serve as your canvas for personal branding. Each post, comment, and interaction contributes to the mosaic that is your digital identity. Be deliberate in your messaging. Craft content that reflects your expertise, insights, and thought leadership. Consistency is key; a cohesive online presence reinforces your credibility.

Authenticity is the bedrock of effective personal branding. Share your professional journey—the triumphs and challenges. Your vulnerability humanizes you, making you relatable and approachable. To truly stand out, inject your unique personality into your online interactions. This distinguishes you from the sea of uniform profiles and resonates with your audience.

Leverage the potential of each platform. LinkedIn, often hailed as the professional networking haven, is ideal for sharing industry-related content, engaging in discussions, and connecting with like-minded professionals. Twitter can be a realm for quick insights and meaningful interactions, while Instagram can provide a behind-the-scenes glimpse into your professional life.

Harnessing Networking Opportunities for Career Advancement

Networking isn't just about amassing contacts; it's about converting those contacts into tangible opportunities. The art lies in nurturing relationships strategically, fostering an environment where collaboration and synergy can thrive.

First, practice the art of active listening. Seek to understand before seeking to be understood. When engaged in a conversation, focus on the speaker, ask insightful questions, and demonstrate genuine interest. This fosters trust and reciprocity.

Second, offer value before seeking it. In the world of networking, the law of reciprocity is your guiding principle. Offer assistance, share knowledge, and provide solutions without the expectation of immediate returns. This builds goodwill and establishes you as a valuable asset in your network.

Third, remember that the value of networking extends beyond the immediate connection. Sometimes, the most fruitful opportunities arise indirectly, through referrals or second-degree connections. Nurture your network not just for immediate gains, but as a long-term investment in your career.

Networking and personal branding are integral facets of your journey toward maximizing income potential. They transform your professional interactions from transactional exchanges into meaningful relationships. By building a strong network, curating an authentic digital presence, and harnessing opportunities with finesse, you'll unlock a realm of prospects that can shape the trajectory of your career and financial success.

Chapter 11: Psychological Aspects of Wealth Management

Emotions and Financial Decision Making

In the tapestry of wealth management, where numbers and rationale often reign supreme, it is often easy to overlook one of the most potent forces shaping our financial landscape: emotions. The human psyche, a complex realm of hopes, fears, and desires, exerts an undeniable influence over our financial decisions, both small and grand. In this sub-chapter, we embark on a journey into the intricate interplay between emotions and financial choices, delving into the profound impact they can wield on our economic trajectory.

The Heart and the Wallet: A Symbiotic Relationship

As creatures of emotion, our financial decisions are inevitably woven into the fabric of our emotional experiences. Whether it's the exhilaration of a successful investment or the trepidation of an economic downturn, our feelings often determine the courses we chart. This symbiotic relationship is neither inherently good nor bad; rather, it underscores the need for a nuanced understanding of how emotions can color our financial landscape.

The Role of Emotions in Financial Choices

It is not uncommon to see individuals making financial decisions that, on the surface, defy logic. The allure of speculative investments promising sky-high returns or the aversion to letting go of underperforming assets can often be traced back to the emotional core. Understanding how emotions influence financial choices is an essential first step toward achieving mastery over our financial lives.

Fear, a primal emotion etched into our evolutionary history, can manifest as a powerful force in the realm of finance. Fear of loss, fear of missing out (FOMO), and fear of uncertainty can lead to hasty decisions, triggering a cycle of buying high and selling low. When market turbulence strikes, fear can amplify the impact, causing individuals to abandon well-constructed strategies in favor of reactionary measures.

On the other end of the spectrum lies greed, an emotion that can cloud our judgment and lead to risky behavior. The promise of quick riches, the allure of speculative assets, and the temptation to chase trends can all stem from a greed-driven mindset. It's essential to recognize that both fear and greed, if left unchecked, can unravel even the most thoughtfully crafted financial plans.

The Art of Overcoming Emotional Biases
So, how can we navigate the stormy seas of emotion and make prudent financial decisions? The answer lies in cultivating emotional resilience and implementing strategies that counter the biases inherent in our psychological makeup.

1. Education and Awareness: Awareness is the first step toward taming the influence of emotions. Educate yourself about common cognitive biases that impact financial decisions, such as loss aversion and confirmation bias. Recognizing these biases in your thought process can help you counteract their effects.

2. Setting Clear Objectives: Establishing well-defined financial goals provides a compass to guide your decisions. When emotions threaten to sway you off course, referring back to your objectives can help you regain perspective.

3. Practicing Mindfulness: Mindfulness, often associated with meditation, can extend to financial decision-making. When confronted with a significant choice, take a moment to pause, reflect, and assess your emotional state. Mindfulness can create a space between stimulus and response, allowing you to make more deliberate choices.

4. Creating a Decision-Making Framework: Develop a structured decision-making framework that involves considering multiple perspectives. Seek advice from trusted mentors or financial advisors who can provide a more objective viewpoint.

5. Embracing a Long-Term Perspective: Emotions can wreak havoc when decisions are driven by short-term market fluctuations. Embracing a long-term view can help buffer the impact of emotional volatility.

Emotional Resilience: A Pillar of Financial Mastery
In the ever-evolving landscape of finance, emotional resilience emerges as a cornerstone of successful wealth management. By acknowledging the power of emotions,

understanding their impact, and implementing strategies to mitigate their influence, we can embark on a journey of empowered financial decision-making. The path to emotional resilience is not without challenges; it requires self-awareness, discipline, and the willingness to confront our emotional biases head-on.

In turbulent times, remember that financial mastery isn't solely about numbers; it's about harnessing the power of emotion to make choices that align with our long-term goals. As we proceed through this book, you'll find that strategies for managing emotions are interwoven into the fabric of each principle we discuss. By mastering your emotions, you are unlocking the gateway to a future where financial decisions are grounded in clarity, purpose, and informed choice.

Mindful Spending and Contentment

In the bustling landscape of modern life, the siren call of consumerism often resonates strongly. Advertisements, media, and societal norms incessantly whisper that happiness lies within the realm of material possessions. Yet, within the realm of prudent financial management, lies a potent truth—true contentment does not emanate from the abundance of belongings, but from the wisdom of mindful spending and the discovery of genuine joy.

Cultivating Contentment Amid Societal Pressures

The world we inhabit today is marked by an incessant drive for more—more possessions, more experiences, and more wealth. This perpetual quest for accumulation can generate a sense of inadequacy, as if the present state is somehow insufficient. It's crucial, however, to recognize that these societal pressures often stem from a narrative of comparison.

Contentment, on the other hand, arises from a profound acceptance of the present moment. It acknowledges that our worth is not measured solely by material possessions but by the depth of our experiences, relationships, and personal growth. Embracing contentment requires a conscious shift in perspective—a deliberate turn away from the external clamor and towards an introspective contemplation of what truly brings us fulfillment.

Differentiating Between Emotional and Rational Spending

In the theater of financial decisions, emotions often take center stage. Emotional spending can be a swift current that sweeps away rationality, leaving behind a trail of impulsive purchases and subsequent regret. Whether it's the allure of a trendy gadget or the temptation of a luxurious vacation, emotional spending can cloud our judgment and veer us off course from our financial goals.

The art of mindful spending entails a mastery of differentiating between emotional and rational impulses. It requires us to pause, reflect, and question whether a purchase aligns with our values, goals, and true needs. By cultivating this awareness, we regain control over our financial choices, ensuring that our money is directed towards endeavors that contribute meaningfully to our lives.

Finding Joy in Experiences Rather Than Material Possessions

In a world that often measures success by the accumulation of possessions, a transformative shift occurs when we reorient our focus towards experiences. Material belongings have a tendency to fade, depreciate, or become obsolete, while experiences possess the magical ability to engrave lasting memories upon the tapestry of our lives.

Finding joy in experiences entails redirecting our resources towards activities that enrich our lives with moments of connection, growth, and exploration. This could encompass embarking on an adventure, engaging in a hobby, or simply sharing quality time with loved ones. These experiences offer a lasting sense of fulfillment that transcends fleeting material acquisitions.

Intriguingly, numerous studies in psychology affirm the value of experiential spending over material consumption. Research shows that the happiness derived from experiences tends to be more enduring and less susceptible to the hedonic adaptation that often diminishes the thrill of new possessions.

The journey of wealth management isn't confined to spreadsheets and investment portfolios; it's an intimate exploration of our relationship with money and its role in shaping our well-being. Cultivating contentment, differentiating between emotional and rational spending, and prioritizing experiences over possessions are integral facets of this expedition.

Psychological Barriers to Wealth Accumulation

In the labyrinth of wealth accumulation, where figures and strategies intertwine, it is not solely the external factors that guide our path. The psychological landscape plays a pivotal role in determining our financial trajectory. This sub-chapter unfurls the tapestry of our inner realm, where money-related fears, self-sabotaging behaviors, and belief systems lay their foundation. As we journey together through these intricate corridors, we will uncover the techniques that empower us to reframe our mindset, paving the way for resounding success.

Addressing Money-Related Fears and Insecurities

Fear is a primal instinct that has served humanity well in navigating dangers and uncertainties. However, when it comes to wealth accumulation, unfounded fears and insecurities can become significant roadblocks. The fear of failure, fear of losing hard-earned money, or even the fear of being judged for one's financial choices can hinder rational decision-making.

Acknowledging these fears is the first step towards dismantling their power. Understanding that fear often thrives in the shadows of the unknown, we can counter it with knowledge and education. Researching, seeking advice from financial experts, and cultivating a deep understanding of various investment options can dispel the fog of fear, empowering us to make informed decisions aligned with our goals.

Identifying Self-Sabotaging Behaviors and Beliefs
Self-sabotage is a perplexing phenomenon—our actions sometimes betray our own best interests. Unraveling the threads of self-sabotaging behaviors requires introspection and honesty. Consider scenarios where you've felt inclined to overspend, to delay savings, or to avoid exploring potentially lucrative opportunities. These actions, often driven by subconscious beliefs, can act as barriers to wealth accumulation.

To identify these beliefs, one must delve into their origin. Were they instilled during childhood, influenced by societal norms, or rooted in past experiences? Recognizing these patterns allows us to question their validity. This is where rationality meets emotional awareness. By challenging these beliefs, we can break free from their grip and pave the way for actions that align with our financial aspirations.

Techniques for Reframing Your Mindset for Success
Reframing the mind is akin to sculpting a new reality—one
that empowers, uplifts, and fosters success. The process of
shifting one's mindset is both an art and a science. It
involves a conscious effort to replace negative thought
patterns with positive, growth-oriented ones. Here are a few
techniques to guide you on this transformative journey:

1. Cultivate Self-Compassion: Be kind to yourself.
Acknowledge that setbacks are part of the journey, and
failures are stepping stones toward success. Self-
compassion encourages resilience and fosters a healthy
relationship with money.

2. Practice Visualization: Envision your financial goals as
if they are already achieved. Visualize the outcomes of
your hard work and smart decisions. This not only keeps
you motivated but also rewires your brain to embrace
success.

3. Affirmations and Positive Self-Talk: Replace negative
self-talk with affirmations that reinforce your financial
aspirations. Phrases like "I am capable of achieving
financial success" can gradually shift your mindset from
doubt to confidence.

4. Embrace Gratitude: Gratitude is a powerful tool that
shifts focus from scarcity to abundance. Regularly
acknowledging the blessings in your life can transform
your perspective and create a more positive relationship
with money.

5. Mindfulness and Present Moment Awareness:
Mindfulness practices help you stay grounded in the
present. This prevents dwelling on past financial mistakes
or worrying excessively about the future. Mindfulness
fosters clarity and rational decision-making.

6. Education and Continuous Learning: The more you
understand about finance, the more empowered you
become. Commit to ongoing education about investment
strategies, financial markets, and economic trends.
Knowledge dispels uncertainty and boosts confidence.

Wealth accumulation isn't solely about numbers—it's about
mastering the psychological landscape that influences our
financial choices. By addressing fears, unearthing self-
sabotaging behaviors, and employing mindset-shifting
techniques, we can transform ourselves into savvy
navigators of wealth. The power to reshape our financial
reality lies within us, awaiting the moment when we step
beyond our psychological confines and embrace the
boundless potential that the world of finance offers.

Chapter 12: Balancing Risk and Reward

Risk Assessment in Investments

In the intricate dance of wealth creation, risk and reward are inseparable partners, each influencing the steps taken on the path to financial prosperity. As we delve into the heart of "The Art of Money," we cast our spotlight on the pivotal realm of risk assessment in investments—a realm where knowledge, introspection, and strategic planning intersect to define the contours of a successful financial journey.

The Dimensions of Risk Tolerance and Investment Horizon

In the world of investments, risk is not a monolith; it possesses shades and dimensions that vary from person to person. Risk tolerance—the ability to endure fluctuations in investment values without anxiety—stands as a foundational pillar upon which investment decisions are crafted. It's a measure of your psychological preparedness to weather market volatility.

Consider your risk tolerance as the vessel that carries your investment aspirations through the seas of uncertainty. Factors such as age, financial goals, and personal circumstances all contribute to the depth of this vessel. A young entrepreneur with a longer investment horizon might be more willing to embrace higher risk for potentially higher returns, while a retiree seeking stability might opt for lower-risk investments to preserve their wealth.

Closely intertwined with risk tolerance is the concept of investment horizon—the span of time over which you intend to hold an investment. Longer horizons often provide the luxury of absorbing short-term market fluctuations, while shorter horizons necessitate a keener awareness of volatility.

The Risk-Return Trade-Off: A Delicate Balancing Act
The financial world operates under the banner of a fundamental principle: the risk-return trade-off. This principle posits that the potential return on an investment is directly correlated with the level of risk assumed. In essence, the greater the risk, the higher the potential reward, and vice versa. This notion is exemplified in the distinction between low-risk assets such as government bonds, which offer modest returns, and high-risk assets such as equities, which present the possibility of substantial gains but also significant losses.

The key to mastering the art of risk assessment lies in discerning your personal comfort level within this trade-off. It's akin to a tightrope walker gauging the tension between the rope's tautness and their own equilibrium. Your unique risk tolerance will shape the composition of your investment portfolio, ensuring it aligns harmoniously with your financial objectives and emotional well-being.

Customizing Investment Strategies Based on Risk Profile
Crafting an investment strategy that mirrors your risk profile is akin to tailoring a bespoke suit—it's a meticulous endeavor that marries your individual contours with the fabric of market opportunities. This journey begins with a thorough examination of your financial goals, risk tolerance, and investment horizon.

For those with a penchant for stability, a strategy focused on income-generating assets such as dividend-paying stocks and bonds may offer a soothing blend of modest growth and security. On the other side of the spectrum, the adventurous souls may navigate the realms of growth investments, venture capital, or cryptocurrency, lured by the siren call of potential exponential gains.

Within this panorama, diversification becomes an invaluable ally. Diversifying across asset classes, sectors, and geographic regions serves as a shield against the ravages of market turbulence. It's the practice of not putting all your financial eggs in one basket—an approach that cushions your portfolio against a single unfavorable event.

In the end, it's not only about the numerical precision of risk assessment models but also about the symbiotic relationship between your head and your heart. A well-crafted investment strategy merges quantifiable data with the unquantifiable nuances of your individual aspirations, tempering logic with instinct.

As we navigate the intricacies of risk assessment in investments, remember that risk is not an antagonist to be defeated, but rather a dance partner that can elevate your financial journey. Embrace risk as an opportunity, and harness its potential to shape a future imbued with the rewards you seek.

The art lies in striking the right balance—an equilibrium where calculated risk and prudent caution converge. It's a dance of patience, awareness, and informed decision-making. As you proceed through this voyage of financial mastery, may your steps be guided by the harmony of risk and reward, leading you towards a future rich in both wealth and wisdom.

Diversification Strategies

In the intricate tapestry of wealth creation and preservation, one thread stands out as particularly vital—diversification. Often hailed as the cornerstone of prudent investment, diversification is not a mere buzzword; it is a strategic approach that can shield your financial endeavors from the caprices of an unpredictable market. In this sub-chapter, we delve into the nuanced art of building a diversified investment portfolio, exploring asset allocation, risk mitigation techniques, and the adaptive nature of diversification.

The Symphony of Investment Diversity

Imagine your investment portfolio as a symphony, where each instrument contributes a unique melody to create a harmonious whole. Diversification is the conductor ensuring that no single note overwhelms the others. At its core, diversification involves spreading your investments across different asset classes, industries, and geographic regions. This mitigates the impact of poor performance in one area by harnessing the strength of others.

Asset Allocation and Risk Mitigation

At the heart of diversification lies asset allocation—a delicate orchestration of resources that can influence the melody of your financial journey. Asset classes—such as stocks, bonds, real estate, and commodities—carry distinct risk and return profiles. Balancing these classes based on your risk tolerance, investment horizon, and financial goals is the crux of asset allocation.

Consider this: during market downturns, bonds tend to be more stable, providing a cushion against equity losses. Conversely, stocks can offer substantial growth potential during periods of economic expansion. By combining these asset classes, you create a resilient portfolio that can weather the ebb and flow of financial markets.

However, asset allocation is not a one-size-fits-all formula. Your age, risk tolerance, financial objectives, and even market conditions should all influence your allocation decisions. The mantra here is adaptability—a diversified portfolio is not static but evolves as your circumstances change.

Navigating the Seas of Change: Adaptive Diversification
In the ever-shifting landscape of personal finance, a static approach to diversification can be limiting. As you progress toward your financial goals and markets evolve, it's essential to fine-tune your portfolio's composition. This process involves periodically reviewing your asset allocation, rebalancing when necessary, and considering emerging opportunities.

Picture diversification as a compass guiding you through unfamiliar waters. As certain sectors thrive while others falter, your commitment to diversification ensures that your portfolio remains anchored and less susceptible to sudden market shifts. Yet, this journey requires a judicious blend of patience and vigilance. Don't hastily chase after the latest market trends, as these can lead to overexposure and erode the protective shield of diversification.

Diversification in Action: A Case Study
Let's delve into a hypothetical case study to illuminate the power of diversification. Imagine an investor, Sarah, who places her entire investment capital in a single industry— technology. While the technology sector is renowned for its innovation and growth potential, it is also notorious for its volatility. If a technological setback occurs, Sarah's entire investment could be in jeopardy.

Now, consider another investor, Alex, who diversifies across various sectors—technology, healthcare, real estate, and consumer goods. During a technology slump, Alex's diversified portfolio may experience less significant losses because the negative impact on the technology sector is mitigated by the positive performance of other industries.

Diversification is the maestro's baton, guiding you toward harmony amid market cacophony. Building a diversified portfolio requires not only an understanding of asset classes and risk, but also an acute awareness of your personal financial landscape.

With careful asset allocation, consistent monitoring, and adaptive strategies, you can forge a portfolio that weathers storms and captures opportunities. The journey toward financial mastery is not one of rash decisions but of calculated, strategic movements. As you embrace the principles of diversification, remember that it's not about scattering your investments arbitrarily, but about orchestrating a symphony that resonates with the melody of your financial aspirations.

Timing and Market Trends

In the intricate dance of finance, where risk and reward are partners, mastering the art of timing becomes an indispensable skill. As we delve into the heart of "The Art of Money," let us explore the nuances of timing and market trends—essentially the rhythm that underscores successful investment decisions.

Analyzing Market Trends and Economic Indicators
In the grand theater of the global economy, trends emerge like currents shaping the direction of financial markets. It's crucial to comprehend that these trends are more than just numbers on a screen—they represent the collective decisions, sentiments, and forces that drive economies forward. To harness the power of timing, one must become adept at deciphering these trends and understanding the economic indicators that illuminate the path ahead.

Begin by establishing a sturdy foundation of economic literacy. Familiarize yourself with key indicators such as GDP growth, inflation rates, unemployment figures, and consumer sentiment indices. These indicators serve as compass points, offering insights into the health and trajectory of an economy. Study historical data, notice patterns, and observe how different economic events impact markets.

When it comes to trends, it's essential to recognize the distinction between short-term fluctuations and longer-term shifts. Short-term volatility can be driven by a myriad of factors—news headlines, geopolitical events, or sudden changes in market sentiment. While these can create opportunities, it's crucial not to base long-term strategies solely on short-term movements.

Strategies for Strategic Entry and Exit Points
Timing the entry and exit of investments is akin to
navigating a bustling city at rush hour—choose the wrong
moment, and you may find yourself stuck in a gridlock of
losses. To avoid this predicament, consider employing
tactical strategies that minimize risk and maximize
potential gains.

One such strategy is Dollar-Cost Averaging (DCA), which
involves investing a fixed amount at regular intervals,
regardless of market conditions. DCA dampens the impact
of market volatility and allows you to accumulate assets at
various price points, effectively reducing the risk of buying
in at a peak.

On the other side of the coin lies market timing, a more
intricate endeavor. Successfully timing markets requires a
blend of research, intuition, and an understanding of
historical performance. Keep in mind that even seasoned
experts find it challenging to consistently predict market
tops and bottoms accurately. Instead of attempting to catch
every market swing, focus on identifying major trends and
aligning your investments with the overall direction.

Recognizing Opportunities in Changing Market Dynamics
Markets are not static; they are living organisms influenced
by a multitude of factors—economic shifts, technological
innovations, and evolving consumer behaviors.
Recognizing these changing dynamics can position you to
capitalize on emerging opportunities while mitigating
potential pitfalls.

One approach is to adopt a growth mindset. Embrace change as an opportunity rather than a threat. For instance, technological disruptions may shake traditional industries but simultaneously open doors to nascent sectors with immense growth potential. Be willing to diversify your portfolio to include both established and emerging industries.

Additionally, keep an eye on global trends that can transcend boundaries and influence various markets. Climate change, geopolitical shifts, and shifts in consumer preferences can create ripple effects across industries, offering perceptive investors the chance to be ahead of the curve.

Mastering the art of timing and understanding market trends is akin to reading the currents of a vast ocean. It requires a combination of knowledge, intuition, and adaptability. As you navigate this ever-changing landscape, remember that while timing is a valuable tool, it's only one facet of a multifaceted investment strategy. The journey to achieving the right balance of risk and reward is an ongoing pursuit, a testament to the artistry that defines the world of finance.

Chapter 13: Financial Empowerment and Education

Empowering Financial Independence

In the intricate mosaic of personal finance, a cornerstone of enduring prosperity lies in the concept of financial independence. It's not just about accumulating wealth, but about achieving a state where your financial decisions are no longer guided by necessity but by choice, where you hold the reins to your financial destiny. In this sub-chapter, we journey into the heart of financial empowerment, exploring the transformative process of breaking free from financial dependency, arming yourself with essential financial skills, and fostering the education of future generations in the realm of financial literacy.

Breaking Free from Financial Dependency

Breaking free from financial dependency is not only a practical goal but an essential mindset shift. It's about shifting from a reactive stance dictated by immediate needs to a proactive position where you dictate the terms. Dependency often breeds vulnerability, making one susceptible to unforeseen changes in circumstances. To achieve financial independence, it's imperative to cultivate the mindset of self-reliance and strategic planning.

Consider this: when you free yourself from the shackles of financial dependency, you regain control over your life's narrative. You become the author of your story, making decisions based on what aligns with your aspirations rather than simply reacting to external pressures. Achieving this independence requires a clear understanding of your financial standing, disciplined savings, and smart investment choices.

Equipping Yourself with Necessary Financial Skills
Knowledge is the sword of empowerment, and in the realm of finance, it's the key to unlocking doors that lead to prosperity. Equipping yourself with essential financial skills not only amplifies your decision-making prowess but also strengthens your ability to navigate the complexities of the financial landscape.

Start by mastering the basics: understanding budgeting, saving, investing, and debt management. Each of these components is a building block toward financial independence. Educate yourself on investment vehicles, risks, and potential returns. Learn about different types of debt and the art of leveraging it effectively. With knowledge comes confidence, and with confidence comes the power to create a solid financial foundation.

Teaching Financial Literacy to the Next Generation
As torchbearers of financial wisdom, we carry a responsibility not only to enrich our lives but also to sow seeds of knowledge that will flourish in the generations to come. Teaching financial literacy to the next generation is an act of empowerment that extends beyond the confines of our own lives.

Consider this act of passing on knowledge as an investment in societal progress. Educated individuals make informed choices, contributing to economic stability and reduced financial vulnerability. By introducing young minds to concepts like budgeting, saving, and investing early on, we empower them to make sound financial decisions from a young age.

As parents, educators, and mentors, we must weave financial education into the fabric of our interactions with the younger generation. Encourage open conversations about money, instill the value of delayed gratification, and introduce them to the magic of compound interest. Teach them to discern between needs and wants, and guide them in navigating the nuances of modern consumerism.

Empowering financial independence is an evolving process—a journey rather than a destination. It's about making intentional choices that reflect your aspirations, having the knowledge to navigate complex financial terrains, and extending the gift of financial literacy to those who will shape the future. By doing so, you not only fortify your own financial security but also contribute to the collective empowerment of society.

Lifelong Learning in Finance

In the intricate tapestry of wealth management, one thread shines resplendently: the commitment to lifelong learning. As we venture into the realm of financial empowerment and education, we peel back the layers of this tapestry to uncover the profound significance of continuous learning in the dynamic and ever-evolving world of finance.

The Imperative of Continuous Learning

In an era marked by rapid technological advancement and shifting economic paradigms, the concept of "learn, unlearn, and relearn" has become a mantra of survival and success. Nowhere is this axiom more relevant than in the domain of finance. The art of wealth management is an orchestration of strategies, instruments, and market trends, all interwoven in a symphony that requires vigilant and astute interpretation.

As guardians of our financial destinies, the onus rests upon us to remain attuned to the ever-changing rhythms of the financial world. Consider this: the investment landscape of today might bear little resemblance to that of a decade ago. New asset classes emerge, regulatory landscapes shift, and disruptive technologies reshape entire industries. Without the willingness to learn and adapt, our financial strategies risk becoming relics of a bygone era.

Embracing the Digital Classroom

The modern world offers a treasure trove of educational resources at our fingertips. The digital realm has democratized learning, opening portals to knowledge that were once accessible only to the privileged few. Online resources, courses, and workshops have become beacons of enlightenment, providing a bridge between financial enthusiasts and expert insights.

Online courses, often designed and taught by industry professionals, offer immersive and structured journeys into the heart of financial concepts. From fundamental principles to specialized topics such as options trading or sustainable investing, these courses cater to learners of all levels. They serve as dynamic repositories of knowledge, where one can grasp the intricacies of portfolio diversification, understand the nuances of tax optimization, or navigate the complexities of derivatives markets.

In the digital age, learning is not confined to textbooks and pre-recorded lectures. Webinars and workshops breathe life into financial education, offering real-time interaction, Q&A sessions, and practical case studies. These virtual gatherings foster a sense of community, connecting learners with industry experts and fellow enthusiasts from around the globe.

Imagine attending a live webinar on the implications of central bank policies on investment strategies, where you can engage directly with economists and investment professionals. Visualize participating in a workshop that simulates stock market scenarios, enabling you to test your decision-making skills in a risk-free environment. These experiences transcend traditional learning, empowering you to apply theory to real-world situations and refine your financial acumen.

Staying Informed in a Shifting Landscape
While formal courses and live events provide structured pathways to knowledge, staying informed about evolving financial landscapes necessitates ongoing engagement with news and analysis. Financial journalism, whether through respected newspapers, dedicated finance websites, or specialized newsletters, offers insights into market trends, economic indicators, and global events that impact investments.

Podcasts, too, have become a valuable source of financial enlightenment. In the comfort of your daily routine, you can tune in to interviews with industry thought leaders, discussions on market trends, and analyses of macroeconomic forces. These auditory expeditions transform mundane commutes or workouts into opportunities for intellectual enrichment.

The pursuit of financial education extends beyond the acquisition of facts; it embodies a mindset of curiosity and adaptability. It is an understanding that the journey to mastery is unceasing, and that every nugget of knowledge, every workshop attended, and every financial news article absorbed contributes to the mosaic of financial wisdom.

Moreover, the act of continuous learning bolsters your confidence and resilience. In a world that often seems enigmatic and capricious, knowledge becomes a shield against uncertainty. Armed with understanding, you are better equipped to make informed decisions, recognize opportunities amid challenges, and navigate the intricate web of financial choices with grace and poise.

As we conclude our exploration of lifelong learning in finance, we are reminded of the age-old wisdom that the more we know, the more we realize how much there is to learn. The financial landscape is an ever-expanding canvas, where every stroke of knowledge enriches the masterpiece that is your financial journey. With each course completed, each webinar attended, and each financial concept grasped, you contribute to the symphony of informed decision-making that orchestrates your financial success.

Mentorship and Guidance

In the tapestry of financial empowerment, there exists a thread that, when woven skillfully, can elevate an individual's journey from mere ambition to resounding success. This thread is none other than mentorship—a profound relationship built upon the foundation of experience, wisdom, and the shared pursuit of financial mastery.

Seeking Guidance from Financial Mentors and Experts
At the heart of every successful financial journey lies a
mentor. A mentor is not merely a teacher; they are a
compass, a confidant, and a source of inspiration. In the
realm of finance, where the intricacies can often bewilder
even the most astute, seeking guidance from those who
have walked the path before is not only prudent but
essential.

Financial mentors are individuals who have weathered the
storms of market volatility, navigated the labyrinth of
taxation, and emerged not only unscathed but triumphant.
Their experiences, both successes and failures, are
invaluable sources of insight for those embarking on their
own voyage to prosperity.

But the significance of mentorship extends beyond the
realm of tactical knowledge. A mentor is a living
embodiment of possibility, a testament to the heights that
can be reached through prudent decisions, strategic
thinking, and relentless determination. Their guidance can
transform uncertainty into clarity and challenges into
opportunities.

Leveraging the Wisdom of Experienced Professionals
In a world teeming with information, the distinction
between knowledge and wisdom becomes all the more
pronounced. While information can be easily accessed,
wisdom—the art of discerning the most relevant, impactful,
and applicable insights—comes from experience. This is
where experienced professionals come into play.

These individuals have faced the complexities of finance head-on, making choices that have molded their own financial destinies. Their ability to distill complex concepts into actionable advice is an asset that every aspiring financial master should seek to harness.

Engaging with experienced professionals offers a dual benefit. On one hand, it provides an opportunity to tap into the reservoir of knowledge accumulated through years of experience. On the other hand, it fosters a sense of camaraderie and community, creating a network of support that can prove invaluable during challenging times.

Providing Mentorship and Guidance to Others in Need
The cycle of mentorship is not confined to receiving; it extends to giving back. As you journey further along the path of financial mastery, you will find yourself in a position to offer guidance and support to those who are just beginning their voyage. This is where the transformative power of mentorship reaches its zenith.

Providing mentorship is not merely an act of altruism; it is an investment in the collective future. By sharing your insights, triumphs, and tribulations, you equip others with the tools they need to navigate their own financial landscapes. Through mentorship, you become a steward of knowledge, ensuring that the wisdom you have gained is passed on to generations to come.

Moreover, mentorship is a two-way street. As you guide others, you deepen your own understanding of financial concepts, refine your communication skills, and gain fresh perspectives that can enrich your own decision-making process. In essence, mentorship is a symbiotic relationship that has the potential to propel both mentor and mentee toward new heights of financial excellence.

In the world of finance, where data and algorithms can dictate decisions, the human element—forged through mentorship—remains the cornerstone of lasting success. Seeking guidance from financial mentors and experts, leveraging the wisdom of experienced professionals, and providing mentorship to others are not isolated actions; they are interconnected threads in the fabric of financial empowerment.

Mentorship has the power to bridge the gap between knowledge and application, turning theoretical concepts into tangible results. It transforms uncertainty into confidence, hesitation into clarity, and aspiration into achievement. As you engage with mentors and fellow seekers of financial mastery, remember that mentorship is not merely a transaction; it is a legacy—a legacy of wisdom, resilience, and the unwavering belief in the potential of every individual to shape their financial destiny.

Chapter 14: Ethical and Sustainable Wealth Management

Ethical Investment Practices

In the mosaic of wealth management, a new paradigm is taking shape—one that transcends the realm of pure financial gain. Ethical investment practices are not merely a trend; they signify a shift in consciousness, reflecting a growing awareness of the interconnectedness between financial prosperity and the well-being of society, the environment, and future generations. In this sub-chapter, we delve into the profound realm of ethical investment practices, illuminating the path towards aligning your financial endeavors with your deepest values.

The Ethical Imperative in Investment

In an era where information flows freely and accountability is demanded, the traditional notion of investment as a detached and purely monetary pursuit is undergoing a transformative evolution. Ethical investment practices recognize that the capital we allocate carries the potential to shape industries, influence policies, and drive change. This recognition gives rise to a profound imperative—the responsibility to ensure that our investments reflect not only financial returns but also positive social and environmental impact.

Integrating Ethical Considerations into Investment Decisions

The integration of ethics into investment decisions necessitates a holistic approach that extends beyond financial metrics. It begins with a deep introspection into your own values, convictions, and the causes that resonate with you. Ethical investment practices invite you to envision the kind of world you wish to contribute to through your financial choices.

Once your values are clarified, the journey entails researching investments with the same diligence you apply to financial analysis. This entails evaluating whether companies align with your values, such as their commitment to environmental sustainability, social responsibility, and ethical governance. Scrutinize annual reports, sustainability initiatives, and corporate social responsibility efforts to gain a comprehensive understanding of a company's ethical standing.

Screening Investments for ESG Factors

Enter the world of ESG—Environmental, Social, and Governance factors. ESG criteria have emerged as a powerful lens through which to assess the ethical integrity of potential investments. Environmental criteria consider a company's impact on nature—ranging from carbon emissions to resource consumption. Social criteria delve into the company's relationships with employees, communities, and the broader society. Governance criteria scrutinize the company's leadership, accountability, and transparency.

The integration of ESG factors in investment decisions creates a multifaceted framework that enables you to gauge a company's commitment to sustainability, ethics, and long-term viability. It empowers you to move beyond the surface of financial performance and delve into the company's ethos and its role as a responsible corporate citizen.

Supporting Companies Aligned with Your Values
Ethical investment practices come to fruition when capital flows towards companies that share your values. By supporting these enterprises, you actively contribute to their growth and amplify their ability to drive positive change. Aligning your investment portfolio with your values acts as a vote of confidence—an endorsement that encourages businesses to prioritize ethical practices and sustainability.

Consider allocating resources to companies that are pioneers in renewable energy, social equality, and ethical supply chains. Seek out industries that catalyze positive transformations, such as green technologies, healthcare advancements, and educational empowerment. Not only do these investments hold the potential for financial gain, but they also create a ripple effect of impact that extends far beyond balance sheets.

In the embrace of ethical investment practices, the boundaries between financial success and social good blur, revealing a nuanced landscape where wealth creation and ethical responsibility intertwine. Ethical investing allows you to be an active participant in shaping the trajectory of industries, fostering innovations that elevate humanity and the planet.

As you navigate the realm of ethical investment practices, remember that your role extends beyond the realm of investor to that of a conscious global citizen. Your financial choices, fueled by ethical considerations, become threads that contribute to the fabric of a more sustainable and just world. By embracing this transformation, you not only build a legacy of prosperity but also a legacy of positive change—a legacy that reverberates through time, impacting generations yet to come.

Leveraging Wealth for Positive Social Change

In the realm of wealth management, there exists a transcendent power—a power that extends beyond personal gain, beyond the confines of balance sheets and investment portfolios. This power is the ability to create lasting social impact, to touch lives, and to leave a legacy that resonates far beyond the realm of finance. Welcome to the realm of social impact and philanthropy—a sphere where financial abundance becomes a vehicle for positive change.

The notion of leveraging wealth for social good has gained tremendous traction in recent years, and for good reason. It is an acknowledgment that wealth carries with it a responsibility—a responsibility to contribute to the betterment of society, to address pressing challenges, and to uplift those who are less fortunate. It is an embodiment of the understanding that financial success need not exist in isolation, but rather, can be a catalyst for broader transformation.

Identifying Impactful Causes and Organizations
The first step in this journey is the identification of causes and organizations that resonate with your values and align with your vision for change. The world brims with worthy causes, ranging from education and healthcare to environmental sustainability and poverty alleviation. Delve into your passions, consider the societal issues that stir your heart, and seek out organizations that are making meaningful strides in those domains.

But how does one discern the impactful from the well-intentioned? It requires a blend of discernment, research, and alignment. Scrutinize an organization's mission, its track record, and the transparency of its operations. Look for evidence of measurable outcomes and genuine dedication to the cause. Engage in conversations with those at the forefront of these efforts—learn about their strategies, challenges, and successes.

Measuring the Social Impact of Your Financial Choices
A cornerstone of effective philanthropy is the measurement of social impact—a process that involves quantifying the change brought about by your financial contributions. This involves going beyond the surface and delving into the

tangible differences your support has made. It requires a shift from anecdotal narratives to concrete metrics.

Consider, for instance, the construction of a school in an underserved community. Instead of merely celebrating the structure itself, delve deeper. How many students now have access to education? What improvements have been observed in literacy rates and overall community development? By asking these questions, you transform your giving into a force that creates lasting change.

Strategic Giving: Beyond Charity to Systemic Change
While charitable donations undoubtedly play a vital role in driving change, there exists a deeper layer of impact—one that involves addressing the root causes of societal challenges. This is where strategic giving comes into play. Strategic giving is a nuanced approach that focuses on systemic change and sustainable solutions.

Rather than solely addressing the symptoms of an issue, strategic giving aims to tackle the underlying causes. This might involve supporting initiatives that empower individuals through education, employment opportunities, or skill development. By targeting systemic change, your contributions have the potential to create a ripple effect that resonates across generations.

The Power of Community and Collaboration
Philanthropy need not be a solitary pursuit—it is often at its most potent when it emerges from a collaborative spirit.

Engage with fellow philanthropists, foundations, and community organizations. Pool resources, share insights, and coordinate efforts to maximize the impact of your giving.

Moreover, consider engaging your family and peers in this journey. Instill in the next generation the values of empathy, responsibility, and the profound joy of giving. Family foundations can become vehicles not only for preserving wealth but also for preserving values and nurturing a legacy of compassion.

As we conclude this exploration into leveraging wealth for social impact and philanthropy, remember that the choice to give is a choice to shape the world. It is a recognition that true wealth extends beyond financial assets to the lives touched, the dreams ignited, and the positive change forged.

Each dollar dedicated to a noble cause becomes a beacon of hope. Each investment in social impact becomes an investment in a brighter future. And as you navigate this realm, may your journey be one of profound significance— one where your wealth becomes a force for lasting good, a testament to your values, and a gift to the world.

Sustainable Wealth for Future Generations

In the intricate tapestry of wealth management, a thread of paramount importance weaves through generations, binding the present to the future. As we delve into the heart of ethical and sustainable wealth management, we encounter a profound juncture—the convergence of responsibility and legacy. In this sub-chapter, we explore the art of nurturing not just financial capital, but also the values and principles that will shape the destiny of generations to come.

Instilling Responsible Financial Values in Heirs

The transference of wealth is not merely a transfer of monetary assets; it is the transference of responsibility. The challenge lies not only in preserving and growing the financial legacy, but also in equipping heirs with the knowledge, values, and discernment to manage that legacy effectively. In this age of instant gratification, imparting a sense of fiscal prudence, long-term thinking, and ethical decision-making becomes paramount.

Fostering responsible financial values starts with open conversations. Engaging heirs in discussions about wealth, its origins, and the principles that underpin its growth creates an environment of transparency. Narrating the family's financial journey, including both successes and challenges, imparts valuable lessons that cannot be learned from textbooks alone. These discussions lay the foundation for heirs to understand the weight of responsibility that accompanies wealth and to forge a meaningful connection to their financial heritage.

Creating a Legacy of Sustainability and Philanthropy: Impact Beyond the Balance Sheet

The legacy we leave extends far beyond numbers on a ledger. It reverberates through the lives we touch and the positive changes we bring about. Ethical wealth management compels us to infuse our wealth with purpose, directing its influence toward the betterment of society and the environment. Philanthropy becomes not just an option, but an imperative—a means to effect change that resonates across generations.

Crafting a legacy of sustainability involves aligning investments and philanthropic efforts with environmental, social, and governance (ESG) principles. This deliberate alignment ensures that the impact of wealth resonates with your values while setting a precedent for heirs to follow suit. Encouraging heirs to actively participate in philanthropic endeavors not only instills empathy and compassion, but also empowers them to continue the legacy of positive change.

Balancing Intergenerational Wealth Transfer with Financial Education

The interplay between wealth transfer and financial education is delicate, for it involves striking a harmonious chord between providing for heirs and preparing them for the challenges ahead. While providing financial security is a natural aspiration, handing down knowledge is equally vital. Empowering heirs with financial literacy equips them to navigate the complexities of wealth and investments with confidence and acumen.

Financial education extends beyond the mechanics of investing; it encompasses understanding the value of resilience, adaptability, and prudent risk-taking. It involves enlightening heirs about the principles that govern markets, the significance of diversification, and the wisdom of seeking professional advice. By striking this balance, you arm heirs with the tools needed to honor the legacy while charting their own course.

As the chapters of our lives unfold, the legacy we leave becomes an enduring testament to our principles and values. Ethical and sustainable wealth management transcends generations, shaping the destinies of heirs who carry the torch forward. Instilling responsible financial values, nurturing sustainability, and imparting financial education are not isolated acts; they are the tapestry of a legacy interwoven with wisdom and purpose.

Chapter 15: The Journey of Financial Freedom

Celebrating Milestones and Progress

In the tapestry of financial growth, marked by myriad decisions and strategic moves, it's all too easy to become consumed by the relentless pursuit of bigger goals and greater achievements. Yet, as we navigate the intricate landscape of wealth creation, it's essential to pause, to breathe, and to celebrate the milestones that pepper our journey. In this sub-chapter, we delve into the significance of recognizing achievements along the way, reflecting on lessons learned from both successes and failures, and the art of sustaining unwavering motivation for the ongoing pursuit of financial growth.

Recognizing Achievements: Beyond the Finish Line

The human spirit thrives on accomplishment. We are driven by the sense of progress, the knowledge that our efforts are bearing fruit. The path to financial freedom is replete with milestones, both large and small, that deserve acknowledgment. These are the moments that propel us forward, providing tangible evidence that our strategies are effective and our goals are within reach.

From paying off a credit card debt to reaching a targeted investment portfolio value, each achievement is a testament to our dedication and commitment. When we pause to celebrate these milestones, we reinforce the belief that our efforts are not in vain. This celebration becomes a bridge between the present and the future, reminding us that every step counts and inching closer to our goals is an achievement in itself.

Reflecting on Lessons Learned: A Journey of Wisdom
In the intricate dance of financial endeavors, not every decision yields the anticipated outcome. Failures and setbacks, though disheartening, hold the seeds of invaluable lessons. Reflecting on both successes and failures grants us access to a treasury of wisdom. Successes highlight strategies that work, while failures illuminate areas that require refinement.

The astute investor recognizes that losses are not defeats but rather stepping stones to progress. Each misstep refines our acumen, enhances our decision-making processes, and fortifies our resilience. When we view failures through the lens of education, we transform setbacks into springboards for future successes.

Maintaining Motivation: The Engine of Growth
The path to financial freedom is not a sprint but a marathon—a journey that demands steadfast commitment over time. It's natural for motivation to waver in the face of challenges or when progress appears slow. This is where the art of maintaining motivation becomes paramount.

Celebrating achievements, regardless of their size, fuels our internal motivation. It's a way of patting ourselves on the back, of reminding ourselves that the journey is worth it.

Moreover, reflecting on the lessons we've gathered, even from failures, amplifies our motivation. We understand that growth isn't always linear; it requires patience and persistence.

The Ritual of Celebration

So, how do we celebrate? Celebrations need not be grandiose; they can take myriad forms. It could be treating yourself to a meal at your favorite restaurant, taking a day off to indulge in a leisure activity, or simply acknowledging your progress in a quiet moment of gratitude. The key is to honor the journey and appreciate the distance you've traveled.

Moreover, celebrate with intent. Set specific milestones that, when achieved, warrant a celebration. This creates a system of positive reinforcement, where the act of celebration becomes intricately linked with progress. It's a way of nurturing your emotional connection to your financial journey, injecting it with positivity and anticipation.

In the symphony of financial growth, celebrating milestones, reflecting on lessons, and sustaining motivation compose a harmonious trio. They fortify us against the challenges, infuse our journey with purpose, and provide the emotional sustenance needed to navigate the complexities of wealth creation. Embrace the art of celebrating not just the destination but the journey itself, for it's in these moments of reflection and appreciation that we truly grasp the profundity of our financial endeavors.

Cultivating a Balanced Life of Wealth

In the pursuit of financial mastery, it is all too easy to become ensnared in the relentless pursuit of wealth, overlooking the treasures that extend beyond the balance sheets and portfolios. As we tread the path to financial freedom, we must remember that true prosperity transcends monetary gains. This sub-chapter, "Cultivating a Balanced Life of Wealth," unfurls before us a tapestry woven from threads of holistic well-being, genuine relationships, and a deep-seated contentment that springs from the heart.

The Pursuit of Balance

The journey to financial freedom demands not just a deft hand at investment and a discerning eye for opportunities but also an appreciation for balance. In our ardor for financial advancement, it is paramount to safeguard against neglecting the facets of life that contribute to our overall well-being. As the cogs of productivity and ambition churn ceaselessly, carving out time for physical health, mental tranquility, and meaningful connections is an investment as crucial as any made in the stock market.

Prioritizing Health: A Precious Wealth

It is often said that health is wealth, and this adage reverberates resoundingly in the realm of financial well-being. A healthy body forms the bedrock upon which all other achievements are built. Yet, in the fervor of chasing financial goals, health can easily take a backseat. Balancing your pursuit of prosperity with regular exercise, nourishing nutrition, and adequate rest is not just a prudent choice; it is a responsibility you owe to yourself.

Remember, the dividends of good health extend far beyond longevity. They manifest in increased energy, enhanced cognitive function, and a robust capacity to navigate the challenges that come your way. Just as you allocate resources to financial investments, channel resources into your physical well-being—it's an investment that pays unparalleled dividends.

The Currency of Relationships

Amidst the hustle and bustle of financial growth, let us not overlook one of life's most valuable treasures: relationships. Genuine connections with family, friends, and peers are the emotional sustenance that nurtures our souls. As you craft your financial legacy, remember that fostering relationships requires time, patience, and sincere effort. Allocate moments to share laughter, engage in heart-to-heart conversations, and lend a supportive hand to those you cherish.

While amassing wealth can be a solitary pursuit, true wealth finds its resonance in the company of loved ones.

Nurture these bonds with care, for they are the threads that weave a rich tapestry of shared experiences and enduring memories.

The Bliss Beyond Monetary Achievements
As financial milestones are achieved and investments flourish, it is easy to conflate monetary achievements with lasting happiness. Yet, the joy derived from material gains is transient, ephemeral—a mere flicker amidst the vast expanse of existence. True contentment emerges not from the digits on a bank statement but from a sense of purpose, a connection with the world around us, and the knowledge that our endeavors have made a meaningful impact.

Embrace experiences that evoke genuine joy—a sunrise shared with a loved one, the feeling of accomplishment after helping others, the quiet satisfaction of contributing positively to society. These moments, intangible and immeasurable, are the true treasures that enrich the tapestry of a life well-lived.

In the grand tapestry of your journey to financial freedom, let each thread of ambition, investment, and strategy be interwoven with the golden threads of well-being, relationships, and contentment. Strive for equilibrium, for it is in this delicate balance that the true essence of prosperity resides. As you continue your odyssey toward financial mastery, remember that the pursuit of wealth is not an end in itself but a means to craft a life imbued with significance, purpose, and fulfillment.

Paying It Forward

In the intricate tapestry of wealth, where figures and forecasts interweave with dreams and aspirations, lies a thread of responsibility that extends beyond personal gain. As we traverse the final stretch of our journey through "The Art of Money," we approach a realm of profound significance—an expanse that beckons us to embrace a role of stewardship, inspiration, and impact. Welcome to the culmination of our exploration: "Paying It Forward."

Sharing Knowledge: Illuminating the Path

A cornerstone of financial mastery lies in the recognition that knowledge is not meant to be hoarded but to be shared. Having traversed the chapters that have illuminated the nuances of financial strategy, the onus now falls on us to disseminate this wisdom. To share the insights acquired, the pitfalls circumvented, and the triumphs celebrated is to be a beacon for others navigating the intricate terrain of finance.

Consider for a moment the pioneers who mentored and guided us along our own journeys. Their willingness to share their wisdom served as a guiding light, illuminating our path and expediting our progress. By passing on our insights, we partake in a tradition that stretches across generations—a tradition of empowerment, where the ladder of knowledge is extended for others to climb.

Inspiration as a Catalyst for Change

In our roles as stewards of financial wisdom, we not only share knowledge but also become wellsprings of inspiration. As individuals bear witness to your journey, your triumphs over adversity, and your strategic maneuvers, they become inspired to embark upon their own odysseys. Your narrative becomes a testament to what is possible when one merges intention with action, and aspiration with strategy.

Being a source of inspiration transcends words—it is the embodiment of a life lived with purpose and intention. When others observe your diligence in the face of challenges and your resilience amidst uncertainties, they are emboldened to believe in their capacity to achieve their financial aspirations. In this way, you become a catalyst for change, fostering a ripple effect that extends far beyond your immediate circle.

Embracing the Role of a Financial Steward

As we delve into the concept of "Paying It Forward," it's essential to acknowledge the broader implications of this role—a role that extends beyond knowledge sharing and inspiration. You become a steward of not only financial wisdom but also ethical conduct, social responsibility, and positive impact. Your choices and actions take on added weight, for they influence not only your own trajectory but also the trajectories of those you touch.

In this capacity, consider how you allocate your resources, how you engage in philanthropic endeavors, and how you align your financial decisions with your values. As a steward, you have the power to guide the course of wealth creation toward endeavors that uplift communities, preserve environments, and drive positive change. Your role as a steward extends to shaping the future landscape of finance, one choice at a time.

As we conclude this exploration, let us reflect upon the tapestry we have woven—a tapestry adorned with principles, strategies, and stories of triumph. Within this fabric lies a strand that illuminates the beauty of sharing, inspiring, and stewarding. The journey of financial freedom culminates not in solitary achievement but in the profound impact we make on the lives of others.

Let us remember that the legacy we leave behind is not solely measured in financial terms. It is a legacy woven with purpose, enriched by the lives we touch and the change we catalyze. As we step into the role of a steward of financial wisdom, let us do so with the understanding that we are part of an eternal continuum—a continuum of learning, growing, and uplifting.

Conclusion: Beyond Wealth—A Lifelong Journey

As we conclude our expedition through the intricate landscape of wealth creation, management, and preservation, it is with a sense of both fulfillment and anticipation that we approach the final pages of "The Art of Money." The chapters within this book have been designed not merely to impart knowledge, but to ignite a transformation—an evolution of mindsets, a refinement of strategies, and an awakening of purpose.

A Continual Journey

The journey of financial mastery is not one with a clear destination but rather a continuum—an ongoing evolution that extends beyond the confines of these pages. As you navigate the paths of entrepreneurship, investment, and philanthropy, remember that each decision you make, each principle you apply, is a brushstroke on the canvas of your financial legacy. The lessons within this book serve as a foundation, but it is your commitment to lifelong learning and adaptation that will truly define your journey.

In the fast-paced world of finance, where trends shift and opportunities arise, the ability to embrace change becomes a valuable skill. Whether you're adjusting investment strategies to align with market dynamics or exploring new avenues of income, remember that the key to remaining relevant is a willingness to learn, evolve, and innovate.

Cultivating Abundance in All Forms

As we delve into the essence of wealth, it becomes evident that abundance encompasses far more than monetary riches. It extends to the richness of experiences, the wealth of relationships, and the depth of personal growth. The pursuit of financial success is most meaningful when it is balanced with well-being, relationships, and a sense of purpose.

Moreover, the abundance mindset—a central theme in our earlier discussions—extends beyond material possessions. It is an attitude that permeates every aspect of life, encouraging gratitude for what you have, fostering generosity toward others, and cultivating a mindset that celebrates possibility rather than dwelling on limitations.

Legacy in the Making

In the grand tapestry of existence, each individual is entrusted with the task of leaving a mark—a legacy that endures beyond their time. As you journey through the intricacies of finance, consider the legacy you wish to create. How will your financial choices reverberate through time? How will your actions shape the lives of those who come after you?

Legacy extends beyond financial inheritance; it is a mosaic of values, principles, and stories that continue to inspire and guide. Perhaps you'll be remembered as a mentor who empowered others to embark upon their own financial journeys, or as a philanthropist who facilitated positive change in the world. Your legacy, like a ripple on a pond, has the potential to touch lives far beyond your immediate circle.

The Intersection of Wealth and Purpose

Throughout this book, we've explored the interplay between wealth and purpose—the fusion of financial success with personal fulfillment. As you continue along your journey, let purpose be the North Star that guides your decisions. When wealth is directed toward endeavors that align with your values and contribute to the well-being of others, its significance deepens. Purpose-driven wealth creation is not only personally satisfying but also contributes to the greater good.

Consider how your financial choices can create a positive impact, whether through ethical investments, philanthropic initiatives, or empowering the next generation with financial literacy. By intertwining wealth with purpose, you transcend the realm of personal gain, venturing into the realm of meaningful influence.

A Grateful Farewell

As our exploration comes to a close, I extend my heartfelt gratitude for accompanying me on this voyage through the artistry of money. The principles, strategies, and stories woven into these pages serve as a compass, guiding you toward financial mastery and a life of purposeful abundance. Your journey is not confined to these chapters;

it extends into the boundless realm of possibilities that await your exploration.

Remember, the pursuit of wealth is not an end in itself but a means to an end—a vehicle that transports you toward the life you envision. As you step into the world armed with newfound insights and fortified perspectives, embrace the journey with enthusiasm, resilience, and the unwavering belief that your financial destiny is within your grasp.

With heartfelt wishes for your continued success,